KNOWING
YOUR INTUITIVE MIND

by Dale W. Olson

Crystalline Publications
Eugene, OR 97402 U.S.A.

PRINTED ON RECYCLED PAPER BY
ECO-BOOKS
EARTH FRIENDLY BOOK MANUFACTURING

MAVERICK PUBLICATIONS
BEND, OREGON 97701

PRINTED WITH
SOY INK

Crystalline Publications

P.O. Box 2088

Eugene, OR. 97402

First Printing August 1990

Second Printing January 1994

Manufactured in The United States of America

ISBN #1-879246-00-7

Library of Congress Catalog Card # 90-83711

Acknowledgements

Special recognition and thanks to Doctor Marcel Vogel, a great scientist, inventor, healer, and teacher. It has been an extraordinary privilege to study under such a wise, loving, and consciously aware human being. He has been an inspiration in broadening my parameters of truth, knowledge and wisdom. His research and development have been a catalyst in bringing our expanded abilities out of the dark ages through applied science. Personally, his light in healing my heart is invaluable and beyond words. His help in igniting the light within will be of great value to many.

I give further thanks to Doctor Rudy Zupancic who has not only been a great friend, but also a great influence and inspiration in showing me that it is Intuition that separates the health care professionals from the true healers.

I would like to give my limitless thanks and love to Judi M. Ferrin for all of her great work in bringing this book into form through her endless love, support, and great design and publishing talents.

Finally, I give special thanks and appreciation to the editors who made this book whole: Elizabeth Scholze, Marge Stoddard, Jodie & Ann Kopp, Carol Alongi and David Johnson.

Cover Design by: Judi Pleskow

Cover Painting, Ocean Sunrise, dye on silk by: Pam Christiansen

Photo Model: Jodie Kopp

Photos by: Peter Johnson

Thanks, I could not have done it without you.

Yeah Team !

Dedication

May this book assist you in Knowing your Intuitive mind, the part of you that is connected to the Infinite source of all Love, Knowledge, and Wisdom.

Table of Contents

Part III
DEVELOPMENT OF THE INTUITION

Part IV
PRACTICE FOR USING THE INTUITION

Note from the author

I am often asked how I became involved in the development of intuitive skills. Over 16 years ago, I found myself entangled in the piles of life's trials. Feeling confused and not knowing the "how to", and the "where to from here", I felt compelled to consult a very wise, elderly "psychic," Johanna Keller. One day, after having had several enlightening sessions with her, she turned to me and said," Dale, you don't need to come to me for the answers, for you have all the answers within you". Of course, I had heard this dozens of times before in numerous books and tapes. Nonetheless, the same old question popped up in my mind, "Yes, but how do you get to that information", or "How do you know when you *know*"? At that moment, Johanna said, "Dale, I'm going to give you two tools to help you find the answers for yourself; the Pendulum and a three-card method for verification". This was the beginning of my work with the intuition externalized beyond my conscious mind. I felt like I was starting at the elementary level. But, for the first time I was able to open communication lines and have direct, conscious rapport with my intuition. In the years that followed, these techniques and others proved to be very precise and accurate in helping me to determine the unknowns not only for myself but for hundreds of others searching for answers to their personal unknowns.

One of the highlights in the development of my intuitive capacities happened over 12 years ago in the Bohemia Mountains of Oregon. This area is not only my favorite camping grounds, but is a region with rich history of gold mining dating back to the Conquistadores. During the Gold Rush era of the early 1900's, 5,000 miners, including many Chinese, swarmed up and down the canyons of the Bohemia Mountains. With nothing more than desire, a set of dowsing rods, a pendulum, and a belief that I too would find gold, I set out to test my intuitive abilities. At the time, I knew absolutely nothing about prospecting, mineralogy, or geology. To shorten a long and adventurous story, by the end of that summer, I had established two hard-rock mining claims and seven placer mining claims amounting to about 180 acres worth of mining operations. I had located not only nugget gold in the river beds, but also gold-bearing quartz veins. Also, I had learned a great deal about prospecting, mineralogy, mining, and geology. The tools of my intuition were dreams, subtle sensing, the pendulum, and dowsing rods that showed me the "Where". My dreams had shown me the idea of mining, and the general area to start. The pendulum assisted me in finding the specific area, depth, and potential amount of gold bearing ore. The dowsing rods indicated the exact point to start digging. Yet, it was persistence, determination, and trust that helped me find what I needed to know. I had fulfilled my desire for an adventure, and found I could successfully use my intuitive capacities to find gold.

During my adventure I learned significant lessons around illusion and visions of grandeur. The incredibly hard work helped to put the deluding effects of gold fever into proper perspective. I never knew there could be so many forms of iron pyrite (fools gold). As they say,

"Not everything that glitters is gold"; a very valuable lesson to keep in mind when making choices that will have long range impact on your life. I did end up with assay reports indicating beyond any question that I had found gold-and silver-bearing ore of a sizable amount, but not of a high enough grade to warrant the exorbitant cost of setting up a mining and milling operation, therefore making the operation financially impractical. At that time, my desire said to go for further exploration, but my intuition was telling me to stop. This great adventure in reality was one of the most dangerous things that I could be doing with my life; working with high explosives, close calls with cave-ins, breathing in quartz dust (which is worse than asbestos), and other dangers. And so my mining operation came to an end out of choice.

The intuition can be a good indicator of when you are getting away from your chosen life's direction for too long, or when you are subjecting yourself to risk that is not for your highest benefit. It took a great deal of strength to put aside my invested interest, desire and visions of grandeur to listen to that small inner voice of my intuition saying "That was a great adventure that you will never forget, and you found what you were looking for". "Now its time to get on with your life's work, and mining for a living is not part of it". "Oh well," I said, "My success is that I have proof that we can use our intuition to learn about something that we have no prior knowledge of, and secondly, we are able to fine tune our capacities to detect the subtle energies of metals such as gold and silver that may be 50' to 150' below the surface of the ground." Now that is quite mind expanding. I didn't fulfill my visions of grandeur or great financial riches. However, it was a rewarding period in the development of my intuition and I will always have fond memories of a grand adventure that made the whole experience very rich.

My advanced work with the intuition as it pertains to the health care profession, has been inspired by Doctors Rudy Zupancic, Benoytosh Bhattacharyya, and Marcel Vogel. After working with Rudy Zupancic for years in his healing practice, I learned effective ways of using muscle testing (Applied Biokinesiology) as an accurate means to intuitively communicate with the patient to access the source or causation of the symptoms, dis-ease, or dis-order.

From Benoytosh Bhattacharyya, I learned that it is possible to diagnose and treat an individual with a dis-order or dis-ease from long distance.

Dr. Marcel Vogel is truly one of the great scientists, inventors and teachers of our times. His work will be reflected in much of the content of this book, the keys being proper use of breath, an open heart and mind, and positive mental-emotional thoughts to bring about health, happiness and harmony in one's life.

After having spent years working with and duplicating their results, I have learned how to use the pendulum, muscle testing, and dowsing rods for advanced forms of multi-dimensional diagnostics of the human body through the use of the intuition. What this means, simply, is that within every human body there is an innate knowledge of everything that is going on within the body, from a complete analysis of the vitamin and mineral content, to deficiencies of any kind, to the exact location and source of all dis-ease. Whether the questioning be of a physical, mental, emotional, or spiritual nature, it is only a matter of the information being available for access to the conscious mind. All information about ourselves is available to us when we learn the art of fine tuning with subtle sensing and our developed intuition.

Doctors Zupancic, Bhattacharyya, Vogel, the author and many others agree that there are four main facets of the human "being:" the physical, mental, emotional, and spiritual, and that all these aspects of ourselves and others can be accurately and completely accessed through the intuition. The magnitude of this work is incredible, and it is definitely worth one's time and determination to become proficient in developing the expanded skills of the mind... the Intuition. Through the development of your intuition, you will find a ten-fold increase in the quality of your life, resulting in greater fulfillment of your mind's potential and an increase in your personal awareness and self-worth. A developed intuition can save time and money, and prevent many of the unnecessary tribulations suffered by those who choose the trial-and-error approach to life. This savings in time and accuracy in problem solving allows for an increase in your health, wealth and the pursuit of your dreams.

Part I

Introduction

We are now in a new age of not only great technological innovations, but also a time with many consciously aware individuals. Our lives are filled with massive numbers of daily choices and decisions which will have an impact on the future of ourselves and others. If we make our choices and decisions completely from our well developed intellect or the five physical senses, then we are limiting our judgement to basically a trial-and-error approach in life.

However, by using the intuition, we may rise above the trial-and-error approach by acknowledging the pool of infinite knowledge. All we need to do is learn the skills to accurately access the intuition.

Our intuition is the liaison or doorway to the Infinite Intelligence. It is through this intermediary that we may draw upon the forces of Infinite Intelligence at will. It alone contains the secret process by which mental impulses are modified and changed into their spiritual or etheric equivalent. It alone is the medium through which thought may be directed into prayer, and prayer may be transmitted to the source capable of answering prayer.

Unfortunately, in this day and age, marketing is more effective in making sales than the actual quality or integrity of a new product or service. Due to this bombardment of choices, it is necessary to develop our intuitive abilities in a practical and tangible sense in order to avoid poor choices which could cost us time, money, health, and a decline in the quality of life.

The labels on products can't possible disclose all the information that you as the consumer may need to know for your well-being. The lack of information, or misinformation, on some products could cost a person their health and possibly their life. With many products, substances and services available these days, we can no longer depend on just our mental mind to make the correct decisions when there are so many unknowns about these products or services

It is no longer necessary to feel the stress that comes from not knowing whether the product that you hold in your hand is toxic, allergenic, non-effective, mildly useful, good, or highly beneficial. However, using the intuition, we can rise above the trial-and-error approach by first acknowledging the pool of infinite knowledge available to all of us. We need to learn the skills necessary to accurately access the intuition.

Many researchers claim that we use only 10% of our brain potential, with some reports claiming that our use is as low as 5%. Although this may sound like a very limited use of our brain, it at least gives us a lot of room for growth. We all have intuitive abilities to see or feel beyond the five physical senses (sight, sound, smell, touch & taste). It is within your abilities to accurately *know* what is or is not for your highest and greatest benefit. The development of your intuitive channels will greatly increase your brain's potential. The ability to use the intuition is very much like learning another skill such as reading, writing, or learning a foreign language. I'm sure you remember how many years of practice and patience it took to develop such skills. The benefits of learning skills to tap the intuition are well worth the effort, and will result in an increase in the quality of life for the person who masters them.

Not using the intuition is comparable to not employing the skills of language, reading or writing. It is possible to get along in this world without these skills; however, the quality of life is greatly diminished. Most people rationalize these abilities away rather than attempting to understand or work on their development. Anyone with a trained mind who has a fairly good ability to concentrate and who has reasonable control over their emotional stability can use these expanded abilities, and can become quite accurate within a relatively short period of time. Remember, we are all born with these abilities of knowing and they manifest in different forms, levels, and degrees. It is a natural ability that you can develop like any other skill, taking only time and practice to acquire. When you develop the intuition, you learn how to use your mind's great potential to the fullest extent.

Throughout this book I refer to "we". I did this, as a result of a certain distaste in using *I this*, and, *I that*, due to my own feelings about a balanced ego. I feel that this book is an eclectic culmination of experiences and knowledge from myself, students in my classes, teachers I've studied with, other authors, and my inner guidance. All of these make up the "we".

Throughout this book, the approach to applying the intuition deals with facts which can be substantiated and verified through objective testing or subjective experience. It is this approach that the author has relied upon and that this book sets forth. For many of us, the use of the intuition means dealing with a whole new way of sensing: a whole new way of acquiring data from the environment. Using the intuition is a new way of using the mind that can take the guesswork out of your daily decisions and choices.

I will take you on an in-depth journey in applying your intuition to assist you in your daily life. In this book I will discuss how the intuition works, how to access the intuition and externalize it with a variety of tools and techniques, and how to develop accuracy in your skillful use of your own intuition.

Chapter 1
KNOWINGNESS

We have all read books or heard talks about our knowingness or our intuitive mind. Throughout this book we will be discussing what the intuition is, how it functions through use of examples, and how to develop our communications between the various aspects of our mind.

There have been many names and categories ascribed to the expanded capacities of the mind, such as the Intuition, Sixth Sense, Knowing Mind, Psychic Mind, Infinite Intelligence, or additional categories such as Knowing, Trance State, Universal Mind, Super-Conscious Mind, or Creative Imagination. All of these categories are basically synonymous in that they come through the same subconscious and conscious interpreting channels of the mind. The source of these expanded states of consciousness can simply be looked upon as the Infinite God lifeforce that dwells in all life.

Defining the Intuition in a literal context, with our limited language, is like trying to explain God. There is so much more on both ends of the spectrum that we don't physically see.

The author looks at accessing the intuition as the ability to have a library card to the big library in the sky, comprised of "all love, all light, all wisdom, and all knowledge of all that is, all that ever was, and all that will ever be". The intuition is the "doorway" through to the Infinite Intelligence, super-conscious mind, the universal mind, and for some, access to the Akashic records. For the sake of simplicity, the source of these many categories can be looked upon as greater and lesser degrees of expanded life experiences with the source, again, being the infinite God[1] lifeforce that dwells in all life. It is the common denominator that rings true in all religions or belief systems. This may be a oversimplification of what the humans on this planet have attempted to define all throughout history. It seems best left to each individual to come to terms with the meaning and definition of the Infinite God lifeforce that dwells in all life.

The outstanding question seems to be, "How do we consciously access, develop, and use the intuitive mind"? How do we apply the ability to use our intuition in a tangible and practical form? Throughout this book the author will answer these questions by discussing many easy-to-apply techniques for externalizing the intuition in a very practical manner. Knowingness of the intuition is a matter of the following eight aspects and attributes.

The Eight Elements of the Intuition are:

- **Ask...** the Infinite part of your being to assist you in your Knowingness.

- **Balance...** of the mental and emotional mind.

- **Intention...** of your objective with clarity.

- **Attention...** to recognition of your intuitive experiences

- **Respond...** to your intuitive experiences immediately. Timing is essential.

- **Trust...** in your intuitive abilities.

- **Persistence...** and determination with Practice.

- **Believe...** your Knowing Infinite Intelligence.

There are many ways to access the intuition with greater or lesser degrees of effectiveness or accuracy. The key is to try many ways, and find one or more methods that are comfortable for you. This probably comes down to which form or tool your belief system allows you to trust. As your personal growth process develops, you may find yourself starting out with one technique for accessing the intuition, only to later switch to another technique that may be faster, more effective, or more complete.

In this book we will explore useful, fun, and powerful ways to use most of the intuitive tools in a very tangible and effective manner. We suggest that you add your own unique qualities to make these techniques work more effectively for you. To begin with, we will cover the more familiar methods for working with your intuition. As we go along, we will assist you in expanding not only your understanding, but also the potential uses of your intuition.

---

[1]The term god is being used to encompass monotheism as well as polytheism, bearing no reflection of the author's beliefs.

Chapter 2
HOW INTUITION WORKS

Resistance to Development

The reason we haven't spent more time in the past developing our intuition is primarily the influence of science, religion, society, and the lack of education. Because the intuition has not been proven through standard scientific means, its validity has been discredited. For most people in this society, science has been the dominating influence on their perceptions of the intuition. Most of us have been indoctrinated to need tangible proof before we are willing to accept a new or different idea. The intuition has not been conclusively proven through empirical study; consequently, our society has been reluctant to accept the concept of the intuition and, in fact, has worked hard at discrediting its validity.

Throughout recorded history, we have openly accepted the validity of a common form of the intuition usually referred to as "mother's intuition". Mother's intuition is a mother's ability to know when something is wrong with her child before any exterior or overt clue has been substantiated. Not every mother experiences this intuition, which may be due to either the lack of attention to such experiences, or, too often, the experience being discarded as a coincidence. However, the majority of the interviewed mothers claimed that they had many such "knowing" experiences with their children.

We all have had the experience one time or another of knowing the outcome of an experience before it happened, and afterwards saying "I knew that was going to happen". Usually we discard such experiences as coincidence. This hindsight of having known the outcome of a particular experience prior to its happening may be very frustrating, especially if a costly or traumatic experience might have been avoided by a quick response to a situation.

The lack of research and development with these expanded abilities of the mind may be due to the perspective of some organized religions which have looked upon the intuition as being less than Godly. Largely it is the fear of the unknown that has prevented this skill from becoming part of our development in our early years of education.

Years ago in school, many of us were reprimanded for what was referred to as "day dreaming". Society's views are changing, and what we use to call day dreaming can be now referred to as creative visualization. We have all experienced day dreaming, and for most of us it is our only conscious connection with the subconscious realm. We now feel it is beneficial to promote and develop this ability at the grade school level. Progressive teachers encourage the development of this ability for good reason which we will go into in greater detail in later chapters.

In the past, there were great misunderstandings around the expanded abilities of the intuition. Most often, these abilities were classified as mysticism or psychic phenomena. In reality, the intuition has nothing to do with mysticism, magic, or the occult.

As an evolving species, we are gaining increased awareness of our intuition and abilities for self-growth.

For many of us, this level of awareness may now equal that of the mystics and healers of ancient civilizations. The only difference is that we are now seeing that these natural abilities are inherent in the majority of today's populace. In addition, many of these abilities can now be verified through sophisticated equipment that is available to measure some of these developed capacities. The scientific community within this country is now starting to give validity and credibility to these inherent expanded abilities of the mind. For the last thirty years, extensive metaphysical research has been conducted by the Soviet Union. Procedures and equipment such as Kirilian photography (etheric energy photography), microvoltmeters (registers electric energy around body), spectrophotometers (optical measurement of light beyond physical eyes), manometers (measuring subtle pressure), and scanners (reading images), have been able to help us see beyond our limited five senses, and to provide verification of these expanded abilities. Along with the innovation of the technologies to test these capacities comes the verification and acceptance of the intuition into the scientific community.

This book is not presented as a thesis to prove or disapprove the existence of the intuition. It is however, directed towards proving use of the intuition. Methods to show exact proof of the intuition through scientific means are still somewhat lacking. Science is still at the stage of technological advancement that has yet to produce equipment that can completely measure the intuition in a tangible form to the satisfaction of the scientific community. This does not mean that the intuition is nonexistent just because it does not meet the standards of one form of measurement. Yet, through subjective and objective testing there has been great evidence to indicate that most, if not all of us, have at one time or another, had what can be classified as an intuitive experience. The scientific viewpoint can be summed up by Jacob Viner, "When you can measure it, when you express in numbers, your knowledge is still a meager and unsatisfying kind".

Whether the intuition has validity for you is something that only you can determine. All that is asked is that you keep your mind open and free from judgement until you have at least experienced the aspects and attributes of the intuition within yourself.

The intuition is the cornerstone of our search beyond the five senses. It is our sixth sense that originates in the brain, and allows us to see-feel-hear-touch-smell beyond our five senses. It is the doorway to understanding our unlimited potential. By expanding these capacities of our intuition, it allows us the ability to "see" beyond the physical sense of the **whole** spectrum. The source of this information or knowledge is available to everyone. With an active intuition, we are on the way to fulfilling our potential.

Knowing When It's Your Intuitive Mind

There are three main indicators to look for when learning to "Know" when it is your intuition:

1. The thought or idea will come into your mind 100% consistent and complete. It will be total in every aspect. It will usually encompass the whole picture followed by all the details. It will answer every single aspect of the dilemma. It will be a complete answer, not a partial or fragmentary answer, and you will recognize it as being an

ideal solution. You will know when you Know, for it will be an "aha!!". It is a space of mind where you just won't question the validity or accuracy of the answers. When you get to this level of the truth beyond the truths you feel very calm and you know or feel that the answers are correct and that there are no more questions.

2. It will be an incredible flash of the obvious. In almost every case, it will be so obvious, so simple, that you will wonder why you didn't think of it before. The reason you didn't think of it before is either it was too early or you were not ready for the answer. When a solution does come that is so crystal clear that it is a flash of the obvious, then you know it is exactly right for you and that the timing is exactly right also. Keep in mind that some of the simplest ideas may be the best. Remember, Keep It Simple Smarty (KISS).

3. You will feel uplifted, a burst of energy, joy, a feeling of elation and excitement, both physically and mentally. This feeling will usually allow you to feel more of who you are. Most intuitive solutions come with energy, inspiration, and excitement that will cause you to want to implement it right now. It inspires you to want to "do" something right this minute. Very often we will get an intuitive solution just before falling asleep, just as we are awakening, or when we are dropping into the alpha state during sleep or meditation, or coming out of alpha as we are starting to awaken. The first hour of the morning is a very important time for stimulating the intuitive mind for expanded creativity. Visualizing your goals first thing in the morning is incredibly important because it is the most powerful time and way to stimulate your intuitive

mind to create. Every time you complete a mental picture of what you want to be, have, or do, it stimulates your subconscious mind into action. That is why it is very important to write down your goals, desires, and questions. Every time you do so, you stimulate your subconscious and intuitive mind into the action of bringing it into form.

Use these indicators of knowing your intuitive mind as a gauge of your intuitive experiences. When you begin your process of developing your intuition, you may feel some of the above aspects and attributes to a very small degree. As you become more proficient with your intuitive abilities you will see these indicators always present.

The feeling experience called *gut feeling* is one of the most common or basic types of psychic or intuitive communications between your conscious and unconscious mind. For example, you're walking down the street and suddenly you have a gut feeling that you are being watched and you turn around quickly to see a very close friend that you haven't seen for a long time walking across the street in the opposite direction. So, you quickly cross the street and stop to talk with this friend and have a mutually beneficial exchange. If you hadn't responded to that feeling you could have missed the experience of meeting and sharing with your old friend.

Another similar scenario is having a gut feeling tell you that you may be in danger from someone watching you who may not have the highest intention. Your gut feeling may be telling you to get away from where you are, and by listening and responding to your intuitive gut feeling you may avoid an unpleasant experience.

Another common form of intuitive insight are *chance encounters*. They are similar to hunches and gut feelings that require conscious recognition. One of the things we find that is true about the intuitive mind is that it sometimes works in a unpredictable and unforeseen manner. Sometimes somebody will call you on the telephone with the solution you need, or sometimes, you will open a newspaper or magazine that you never read and there will be an article with an answer or solution. You may meet someone casually who will make a suggestion that will turn out to be the perfect solution to the major dilemma, challenge, or goal that you are attempting to accomplish. Be alert to the people you run into who may have the solutions. Be alert to written material you come across that may contain the answers, because invariably the answers come in ways that may be totally unexpected, not in the ways you would logically expect them to come. This is sometimes referred to as *synchronicity*, which means a phenomenon when several seemingly unrelated events occur to form a pattern or solution for a particular problem that you were working on. We have all had such experiences in which hindsight has shown how unrelated events worked together to make up the whole picture in solving a major life challenge.

It takes practice to develop your ability to listen to this subtle input, trust in this ability, and learn how to utilize it by responding to it. The more you direct your **attention** to this part of your life, the more frequently the feelings come and the more your intuition develops. Most people tend to analyze or rationalize these experiences away rather than attempting to understand them or work on development of these abilities. You will find that the more rapidly you respond to these intuitive insights, the more intuitive experiences you will have. Trust in your intuitive ability and respond to it immediately. Successful people, regardless of lack of education or level of intelligence, have become successful due to their ability to use the intuitive mind and to respond immediately to it, and have reaped great benefits by plugging into the Infinite Intelligence of the intuitive mind.

It is easiest to experience the intuition when the conscious mind is either completely focused or defocused. Most often the intuitive mind works best when the mental mind is working 100% in concentration on solving the problem or in achieving the goal. Often times when you are completely focused on the goal, desire, or objective, the ideas will flash in your mind. Other times, the intuitive mind will come through with a flash when the conscious mind is completely elsewhere... thinking of something totally separate or apart from the problem or goal that you are working on. For example, you may be driving along, going for a walk, listening to music, in the middle of a conversation, or for many, taking a shower, and suddenly the idea or the answer that you have been searching for will shoot into your mind with crystal clarity. The intuitive mind does not work when you are mulling over your problems or goals. Intuition works when concentrating totally, or not at all. Try both on every plan, idea, or goal when you would like the answers from your Infinite Intelligence. It is a matter of just asking the intuitive mind for answers, then waiting as you are going about your business driving your car, or taking a shower, etc... and let the answer come into your conscious mind. The intuition will have exactly the right answer required to solve your problem or achieve your goal at exactly the right time for you. It is simply a matter of *trust* and *timing*. Your intuitive mind knows the best time better than you do (conscious mind), and the most important thing to do when the answer comes to you is to act on it immediately. You must immediately implement the flash of insight or the idea or the answers that come to you. Many times, when we have a flash of an idea and we say "I will get on it in the morning," and then when we act on the thought, it may be too late. So when you have a intuitive flash in regard to your goal, it is essential that you act on it immediately without hesitation, because sometimes you can be seconds away from being too early or too late.

Part II
UNDERSTANDING YOUR INTUITION

Chapter 3
ENERGY, THE BRAIN & THE INTUITION

Energy: the Source

We live in an energy universe. Every organism is surrounded by all kinds of energy. Some energy is beneficial and some is utterly destructive. This energy can be seen through the technological advancement of Kirilian photography which shows a type of electrical energy emanating around all life forms. Our bodies basically operate on an electrical-magnetic form of energy. Only a few years ago, science for the first time was able to isolate a single cell from the human body, which, in a way, resembles a battery possessing both a positive and negative ± terminal. It is a fact that our bodies and minds function as result of an electrical energy system, even though the electricity can not be seen by the physical eye. The electrical and magnetic nature of the human body with its extraordinary processing potential could easily be likened to a combination computer, radio, and television.

To survive, every organism has developed means by which it can sense the more harmful energies so that it can avoid them or protect itself The famous experiments by Cleve Backster and Marcel Vogel have proven that plants will shrink away from people who radiate hostile energy toward them. Animals too, sense when danger is near. Even humans will flinch or draw back from a painful or unpleasant sensation. All living matter has an innate intelligence which manifests in a kind of "primary perception" of what is helpful or harmful. Humans have a highly developed ability to sense this energy, although most of us are generally unaware of this perception in our daily consciousness. Our over-identification with our intellectual faculties may cause us to ignore this sensitivity and miss what is happening at these higher and more subtle levels of awareness.

Even though there are many ways of communicating intuitively, the essential nature of the intuitive part of the mind remains the same. The source is energy. It initiates both light and sound through the movement of atoms in space. From the source comes vibratory currents of energy producing life in all forms, thereby creating our energy universe. Everything that is going on in the world today, all circumstances, all events are a function of thought created by energy. Our intuitive perception and everything in our reality is based on energized vibrations. Everything, including yourself, is made up of energized atoms vibrating at a specific frequency that is unique only to you. As you begin to look at life from this perspective, you will see with greater depth what motivates people, and how the energy works with total understanding. As a result of this understanding you may look at yourself and others in terms of energy.

Creativity is the release or expression of energy. This creative self expression is empowering. By making use of your creative imagination and your energy, your reality becomes of total choice. You choose to create your own communication system, what you listen to, what programs you run, what thoughts, feelings or words you express. The intuition works best when you have deliberate and conscious thoughts on how you want to use your creative energy. If you choose to recognize only the physical world as reality, you deliberately cut yourself off from conscious intuitive communication. When you do choose to be conscious of a fuller reality, and you choose to recognize your intuitive mind as being valid, it will begin to communicate with you.

There are many ways in which we communicate on the intuitive level. Some of these ways we may not even be aware of, even though we may be using these abilities on a daily basis and dismissing many of the obvious experiences as coincidental. Sometimes even the most intuitive people don't recognize their abilities, nor do they always know how to channel them or use them in a tangible and practical form.

Where the Intuition Resides: The Brain

In order to understand the function of the intuition and where it resides within our brain, we first need to explore some of the various aspects of the brain itself. The brain that we carry around with us has incredible capabilities of a magnitude that we are just now starting to recognize. The left part of our brain may be impressed with what today's computers can do, however, these computers do not compare to the capacities of the human brain. Some researchers have observed that in many ways, our brains are far superior to any computers yet designed. The human brain is three pounds of mystery: only 2% of the body's weight, it uses 20% of the blood and 25% of the oxygen supply. Estimates of the number of its neurons range from 20 to 100 billion, with 100 trillion to 500 trillion neuronal connections (synapses). Over a hundred million bits of information pour into our brains every second, and the brain scans itself every one-tenth of a second, operating on some 20 watts of power. It receives, evaluates, and processes information. It makes decisions, sets goals, initiates actions, and creates. Our brains are capable of a great deal more than we've been taught to imagine. We need to be reminded from time to time of our brain's great processing potential which far exceeds the electronic capabilities of computers, radios, and televisions of today.

The transmitting stations of the energy that we intuitively perceive are the objects or individuals themselves, which are continually broadcasting or radiating energy frequencies. Frequency means cycles per second that a particular object or individual's energy vibrates. The higher the frequency the finer the vibrations, the lower the frequency the denser the vibrations. Every object, plant, animal, or human being on this planet has an energy that vibrates at a specific frequency that is unique only to itself. Nothing has exactly the same frequency. It is these energy vibrations, and learning how to "subtle- sense" the different frequencies, that make up the software of the intuition. The software of the intuition is the application, or program being used to access various pieces of information through the hardware, the physical part of the brain.

The mind operates something like a combination of computer, radio, or television receiver and transmitter. In this day and age everyone is familiar with radio band and TV frequencies, which makes the following principle easy to understand. **Intention** and **concentration** are the tuning devices, or software, of the mind. Learning to develop your intuition requires using your software by concentrating your intention on that which you wish to do, be or know. Your thoughts are a form of energy. Your thoughts concentrated on a definite purpose will create certain results. A person with a properly trained mind who can concentrate and hold their thought on a particular object, idea, person, substance, or concept becomes tuned in to that frequency. Nerve cells begin to vibrate in resonance to it, and this vibration has a frequency and wavelength which gives it a unique quality, tone, or color. The nervous system of the human body then translates this quality or frequency resonance which is then transferred to a conscious knowingness, or subtle-sensing.

Most people have had the experience of communicating with another person on the non-verbal or Intuitive level. This form of communication is processed through the electrical components of the body, and is accomplished by a means that is similar to that of a CB (Citizens Band) radio, with each of us having a particular frequency (call letters) which no one else on this planet has. It is this connecting with the frequency of another person through *focused intention* that makes the intuitive experience. I'm sure you have heard of experiences such as a mother "hearing" her child cry out for help, and arriving in the nick of time to help save her child. This would be an example of what is referred to as *clairaudience*; the mother could not hear the child with her physical ears, yet she could *hear* the crying out of her child.

One of the most common intuitive communications, which you may have experienced many times, is when you have answered someone's question, and then realized that the person hadn't said anything yet. Or after you answer, the person you have been talking with says, "I was just going to ask you about that!" Other examples include walking over to the telephone just before it rings, or knowing who it is on the telephone when you hear it ring, or getting a picture of the person calling in your mind as the telephone rings. Again, these are common non-verbal or intuitive communications that many of us discard as coincidence. These are examples of intuitive abilities that we need to recognize in order to consciously communicate with the intuition. One of the main problems that occurs with attempting conscious reception of these non-verbal communications is when there is too much "static" or mental-emotional interference. For proper intuitive reception, interference either within our brains or from within the environment needs to be taken into consideration. Understanding the difference in communications between the vibrations from your inner intuitive mind and the vibrations from the outer expressions of other life forms is the challenge that everyone faces in their development of the intuition. Nonetheless, the following examples of non-verbal communications clearly indicate that intuitive communications reside in an area of the mind apart from the intellect. Regardless of a limited or impaired intellect, the intuitive communications are still 100 % available.

While working with mentally retarded children, the author discovered that most often the children would respond to nonverbal or telepathic communications in reference to things that they would like. This response occurred despite their individual mental handicaps. For example, they might respond to a mental image of playing in the park, or feeding the ducks, or attending an ice cream parlor, or a dynamic music show. The important point here is that, regardless of intellectual handicaps, these children could still access that part of the brain that received these intuitive responses.

Try the following experiment with children from the ages of 4 to 10 years (most receptive). Use a non-distracting (neutral) room, with a child that you are very close to. Create a complete image of a bowl of chocolate ice cream (or the child's favorite treat). Hold that clear image in your mind for a few minutes. Now incorporate the feeling of desire with that image while closely observing that child's facial expressions or actions, and continue to hold that image with the feeling of desire with the greatest of detail for another few minutes. Most often, when questioning a child after a few focused minutes of this image mixed with desire, you may find the following response: "Would you like some chocolate ice cream? Yes!!! Were you thinking about ice cream? usually, Yes!!!"

Another experiment that you could try with your pet animals (dogs and cats work best), is to picture your pet's favorite activity, like going for a walk or a food treat that they really like. Hold that image, and now add the emotion of desire with all detail and watch them come running. This may take some patience and persistence, but many times we have seen these tests work on the first try. These are examples of how expanded levels of communication, focused intention, and imagery mixed with emotion, can occur without the mental interference of the left-brain ego.

Communications Site

In order to understand the function of the intuition, we need to clarify some of the attributes of the human brain and how we perceive intuitive communications. To function, the intuition relies on the synergy, or working together, of several different mechanisms. The brain, the endocrine gland (pineal & pituitary) hormones, the nerve cells, the life force from the breath, and the muscles, all must work together to create the intuitive response.

The human brain is basically divided into two hemispheres which have distinctly different qualities and purposes. In western society we rely on the rational or left part of the brain almost to the exclusion of the right, or creative-intuitive, side of the brain. For most of us, this means our lives are filled with goal-oriented, action-oriented, linear, logical, analytical, verbal thinking. The left-brain focused individual concentrates on the personality, mathematical functions, desires of the ego, time, and the sequential series of events: today, tomorrow, the next day.

Because we live in a left-brain society, accessing our intuitive capabilities can be difficult. In order to free up the use of the intuitive capacities, it seems necessary to appease the logical left brain with enough believable or acceptable information about the basis and validity of our expanded intuitive realities. This left-brain dominance usually leaves us with a sense of imbalance, incompleteness, and a feeling of being unfulfilled; a sense that "something is missing". Perhaps that is why you chose this book.

Although many of us have been frustrated by this left-brain, rational-logical approach which disregards the intuition, we do have an innate desire to experience all aspects of ourselves. When we are primarily using the right side of our brain we are creative; feeling, inspiration-oriented, imaginative, spatial, timeless, and intuitive. A right-brain individual will tend to be more directed by inner impulses or motivated by the higher intuitive self. The right-brain focused individual usually acquires some conscious awareness of universal truths thus gaining the perspective of seeing the common denominators true in all realities.

In this society, these right-brain attributes have been tremendously undervalued, and in some cases totally ignored. The important perspective for now is an awareness of the differences between right and left brain hemispheres, and the various aspects and attributes associated with each. In which side of the brain do you spend most of your time? As Ernest Holmes said,"Where the mind goes is where the energy flows." By concentrating on something you empower it. With focus on the right side of the brain, you begin to stimulate your intuitive awareness that allows you to develop a knowingness in how you live your life. You enter into a greater knowingness, a greater understanding of how energy flows in all the things around you.

The intellectual capacities of the left-brain *can* assist us in finding the correct answers in life. But, because our left-brain capacities are largely over developed, they can drastically interfere with our intuitive capabilities. Relying solely on our left-brain intellect leaves us imbalanced, and closed off to other options. That is one reason why it is important to be able to "defocus" or put the intellect to one side when doing work with the intuition and the higher aspects of consciousness. Another reason is that along with the intellect there is also the ego. The ego has a vested interest in the outcome of the answers, and thus has a tendency to get in the way of accurate, objective, intuitive answers. The ego or intellect will be discussed further in the section on the subconscious mind.

People who have done a great deal of work on themselves in the area of self growth will have inevitably moved from a left-brain focus to a right-brain focus, meaning that they have moved from being totally dependent on the intellect as a motivating force, to a lifestyle that is based more on feeling and intuitive "Knowingness". You will find this type of person will accept experiences more easily and readily, being much more open, and in touch with who they truly are. The quest since the beginning of time has been, "KNOWING your true self". The intuition will help you to discover your inner truths and facilitate healing and rebalancing within all aspects of your daily life.

Chapter 4
DEVELOPING THE INTUITION

Conscious/Subconscious Mind

Everything that we create first begins in the form of a thought. We can create nothing which has not first been conceived in thought. Through the aid of the imagination, thought impulses may be assembled into plans. The imagination, when under control, may be used for the creation of plans or purposes that lead to the success in one's health, relationships, occupation, and material wealth. Thought impulses, created in the conscious mind via the imagination, are transferred to the subconscious mind to be brought into form. Einstein once said, "Whatever you can hold your interest on completely for at least four minutes, you can bring into form (physical reality)".

The first and most important step in developing the intuitive mind is to remove the thought of "coincidence" or "by accident" from your vocabulary and to refrain from rationalizing your intuitive experiences away. By removing the invalidating words "coincidence "and "by accident" from your vocabulary, you open the door to the subconscious mind, home of your intuition.

The subconscious mind is the interface or the integrated connection between the conscious mind and the intuition. With practice, the intuition becomes a more conscious part of the mind in this interplay between the unconscious and the intuition. This is what is referred to as being consciously aware, consciously conscious, or enlightened.

When ideas or concepts flash into one's mind through what is popularly called a "hunch" or "gut feeling," they come from one or more of the following:

- Infinite Intelligence;

- One's subconscious mind, where every sense impression and thought impulse which has ever reached the brain through any of the five senses is stored.

- From the mind of some other person who has just released the thought or picture of the idea or concept, through conscious thought;

- From another person's subconscious storehouse.

There are no other known sources from which "inspiration" or "hunches" may be received. There is plenty of evidence to support the belief that the subconscious mind is the connecting link between our finite or conscious mind, and our intuition or Infinite Intelligence.

Inhibitors and Developers of Awareness

Nature has built humankind so that we have absolute control over the material that reaches our subconscious mind through our five senses. This is not meant to be construed that we exercise this control. However, it does mean that *the only real control over our lives is through our thoughts and words.* Our subconscious mind functions involuntarily, whether we make any effort to influence it or not. This suggests to us that both positive and negative thoughts serve as stimuli to the subconscious mind, even though the negative thoughts such as fears, guilt, shame, doubts, angers, and resentments are the most destructive to our lives. In acquiring mastery over our negative impulses, we give the subconscious mind more desirable food to be nourished by, and thus transform health and happiness into our realities. Again, *the basic operating principle of the subconscious mind is:* **any thought, plan, idea or goal held consistently in the conscious mind must be brought into the reality of our lives by the subconscious mind, whether positive or negative.** This is why it is so important to keep our minds focused in a positive way, and to talk, think, and imagine only that which you desire to bring into your life. Our lives are filled with nothing more than what we continually think about in our minds and feel with our hearts.

A successful person will rigorously keep their mind focused on that which they wish to bring into their lives rather than on what they fear. If you constantly think of that which you fear or that which you don't want in life, you will, in fact, attract it to you. **Like attracts like!** Therefore, it is for your greatest benefit to **not** constantly talk, think, write about, or dwell upon the things you fear. Any thought, plan or goal held in your mind on a continuous basis will at one time or another be brought into reality. You are able to be in complete control of what you manifest into your life. By holding desire and determination of that which you want to attract into your life long enough, it **will** come into reality. It is the Law of Attraction that will bring about this success. It may seem like a lot of work to consciously manifest such positivity into your life. For some, it may even seem a struggle due to poor indoctrination by society. This is not to be taken personally as a character defect. It takes time and effort to reprogram the conscious and subconscious mind toward empowering positivity, yet the rewards of an increased quality of life are well worth it. Know beyond any question of doubt that it is your birthright to be happy, healthy, wealthy and whole. To learn and integrate these attributes into your life will not only make for success with your work with the intuition, but it will bring success into every part of your life.

We are living daily in the midst of thought impulses which are reaching our subconscious minds, with or without our conscious awareness. Some of these impulses are negative, some are positive. Working diligently to shut off or limit the flow of negative impulses, and voluntarily influencing your subconscious mind through positive impulses, will bring into your life your, **health, wealth, love, perfect self-expression, joy, peace, harmony, clarity, and prosperity.**

While studying with Marcel Vogel, we conducted an experiment that showed us a great deal about the power and substance of thought. A group of 60 health care professionals was gathered for this experiment. The objective was to raise the vibrational energy field within the room that we occupied by using our minds and heart centers. In other words, we as a group were attempting to increase the level of heartfelt Love energy within a group setting by means of intended focus of all the individuals within the room. This experiment was being measured with an Omega 5 energy sensing device, and subjectively by all 60 of us monitoring the change with our own subtle sensing abilities. To summarize the findings, as a group we built the measurable energy field up from 225 units to 2650 units within a period of 15 minutes. Everyone within the room could feel this increase in love energy beyond any question of doubt. It was a happy, warm, peaceful and fulfilled heart sense. Then Marcel walked in and just stood there for a minute directing his right hand in a sweeping motion towards all of us in the room and walked out not saying a word. The energy in the room completely shifted. We measured the room again and found the rating had dropped down to 350 units; the feel of the room was as it had been at the beginning of the experiment, and mostly void of all the heartfelt energy that the group had created. Marcel walked back in, went over to the blackboard and wrote, *"A Negative or Critical Thought, Be It Conscious or Unconscious WILL Neutralize a Positive Effect or Outcome"*.

This was an interesting experiment with group dynamics, showing not only the effect that a group can have on the environment when it is single mindedly focused, but also what one person can do to disrupt this energy level. Of course, most people are not able to have that dramatic an impact on a group. Nonetheless, it does indicate how we can be affected by our own and other's thoughts. Thoughts are tangible and can have very dramatic effects on ourselves and others.

Positive Subconscious Expansion

The subconscious mind consists of a field of consciousness in which every impulse of thought that reaches the conscious mind through any of the five senses is classified and recorded. It receives and files sense impressions or thoughts, regardless of their nature, for the subconscious mind takes everything completely literally. The subconscious mind does not know when you are joking, it only registers the thoughts or words. You may voluntarily plant in your subconscious mind any plan, thought, or purpose which you desire to translate into its physical equivalent. The subconscious acts first on the dominating desires which have been mixed with emotional feeling, such as love, joy, laughter, or anger, sadness, grief, sorrow, depression, and anxiety.

Remember, *the subconscious mind may be voluntarily directed through habit, under the direction of your conscious mind through positive spoken words, thoughts, and positive environmental stimuli.* **Be Patient, Be Persistent.** The key to opening and changing the negative patterns or habitual thoughts of the subconscious mind can be accomplished by persistently replacing them with positive thoughts, words, and environmental stimuli. Through the focused exercise of these forms of positivity, one gains insight into how the subconscious is influenced and can then monitor what goes in and ultimately what comes out of the subconscious. Creating a positive conscious and subconscious mind will be discussed later in further detail.

The attribute of persistence is something that will be coming up over and over again throughout this text. Persistence is one of the main keys to success in developing the skills of the intuition.

> *Persistence is an essential factor in the procedure of transforming desire into its intuitive or knowing equivalent. The basis of persistence is the power of will.* ***Will-power and desire, when properly combined, make a powerful pair.***

Unfortunately many people are ready to "throw in the towel" and give up at the first sign of opposition, or failures, or an apparently wrong answer. Successful individuals carry on despite all opposition until they attain their goal, or the correct answers. In the development of the intuition, the author found many hurdles to get past, but these obstacles have proven to be his friend. In the process, he discovered that: *We learn and grow more from our failures than we do from our successes.* In thousands of inquiries throughout the development of his intuition, the author has had a few hundred intuitive experiences that could have appeared as wrong answers, and, in some cases it was, in fact, wrong. More often the fault lie not in the intuition, but in asking the wrong questions, or failing to adequately set up the questions with the proper time and place factors. Nonetheless, the ego or intellect can be so quick to jump in and say, "See, I told you that stuff isn't true", or "That intuition stuff is only a 'figment' of your imagination". Gently thank your left brain for its concern, continue to trust your intuition, and remind your left brain that, it too, has sometimes been inaccurate. Be Persistent!

Persistence is a major key for the development of the intuition. It is only through habit and persistent feeding of positive thoughts, affirmations and feelings to our subconscious mind that we will achieve complete mastery of our emotions, mind, and the intuition.

Creating a Positive Mind

The possibilities of creative effort connected with the subconscious mind are stupendous and limitless. The intuition can inspire one with a feeling of awe for it is truly Infinite.

Once again, the subconscious mind takes any orders given it in a spirit of absolute faith, and acts upon these orders. Most often the orders have to be presented over and over again, through repetition before they are interpreted and completely accepted by the subconscious mind. *What you think, what you speak, you become.* Auto-suggestion or affirmation is the means of control through which you may voluntarily feed your subconscious mind thought forms of a creative nature. By neglect, you permit thoughts of a destructive negative nature to find their way into this rich garden of your mind. The author has known of many people who have cured themselves of terminal cancer and others who created a world of material wealth through the assistance of positive thoughts and affirmations.

Louise Hay in her book You Can Heal Your Life gives a fine demonstration on the use of positive affirmations and the healing powers of our infinite minds. If you find yourself with constant negative thoughts, then it will be necessary to fill the mind with equal or greater positive thoughts and emotions in order to rebuild the subconscious mind to bring about healthy or positive intuitive abilities. Many of us have had thousands of negative thoughts or words toward and about ourselves. This will be how many times one needs to use the method of positive thoughts or affirmations in order to balance out the negative programming of the subconscious mind. For some of us, it would mean finding the appropriate affirmation or affirmations and saying them over and over at least a few hundred times throughout a day, every day for at least a month. One affirmation from Louise Hay that we have found to be very effective in restoring one's personal power and rebuilding one's emotional stability has been, "I Love and Approve of

Myself". We have given this affirmation and similar ones to hundreds of our therapy clients, and have seen great results. Find the affirmations that feel most appropriate for you and use them with persistent effort to bring about whatever positive change that you need in your life. Other affirmations that we have found to be helpful are:

- I now release the past and allow love to heal every area of my life.

- I Am worthy of the very best in life and I now lovingly allow myself to accept it.

- The answers within me come to my mind with ease.

- I Am always under direct inspiration. I know just what to do and give instant response to my intuitive leads.

- There are no mysteries in the Kingdom. Whatever I need to know will now be revealed to me, under grace.

- It is safe to see and experience new ideas and new ways. I Am open and receptive to all good.

Chapter 5
EMOTIONAL AND MENTAL BALANCE

To achieve effective and accurate work with the intuition, it is essential that one be emotionally and mentally balanced and centered. By emotiojnal balance we mean a state of emotional harmony; neutral feelings neither too high or too low, but centered. This means your thoughts need to be centered and positive without attachment to the outcome, and without any critical or judgmental thinking toward yourself or others. Now we will work with techniques that can remedy these imbalances easily and instantly.

We do know that the intuition is not dependent on the intellect. In fact, the intuition is dependent on our ability to be able to put the ego or intellect to one side long enough for the right or intuitive brain to get through to our conscious awareness. In other words, *the intuition must come through the filters of the conscious mind to its final stage, the conscious thought. Along the way, accuracy of content can be altered by either the intellect-ego or negative emotions, thereby creating doubt or lack of trust.*

Intellect-Ego

The two components of the conscious mind are the emotional mind and the mental mind. The mental, intellectual or rational part of our mind acts as an inhibitor that is capable of cutting us off from the inner dimensions of our knowingness or infinite intelligence. It is the ego part of our mind, the intellect, that can be the great inhibitor of the intuition. Like the ego, it is the caretaker of the mental mind, always rationalizing to create a protected comfort or safety zone for the intellect. There is nothing wrong with having a well developed intellect. It has its place and purpose. But when the intellect gets in the way of the intuition there is a problem, for it can readily cut us off from all the inner dimensions. It is that part of the intellect or the ego that fears to experience or do something without previous knowledge. The ego is invested in things being just the way they are and does not want to face unknowns. This is why it will defend its position by insisting on sticking to the facts and figures of what is known so that it won't be wrong. This inhibiting factor of the ego exists because we don't want to make fools of ourselves. We don't want to be wrong. It is that part of ourselves that doesn't know if the messages coming from the inner mind are true, or it's not sure where this information comes from. This can, in fact, undermine one's trust or faith and can deter the development and/ or accuracy of the intuition. We have talked with many people who have well developed intuitions, and the most commonly stated experience for most have been: "Even though I have been consciously using my intuition on a daily basis for years making accurate decisions and choices, once in a while I still wonder about it".

We are a well indoctrinated left-brain society, and it will take time and individual effort for change in conscious awareness. When working on developing your intuition, just be aware of the thoughts that surface. When you find yourself in a state of doubt about your intuition, ask yourself whether these thoughts are latent fear coming from the ego. It is healthy to remind your intellect of how many times it has been incorrect in decision making, and that it is okay to allow the intuition to assist in making more accurate decisions and choices.

We would like to share with you a story about a man named Chuck, who was a medic in Viet Nam. His mind would not allow him to carry a weapon. His body would actually seize up if a rifle was placed in his hands. However, he found that he had talents that surfaced during his tours as a medic. He discovered that he was able to know when, and where, not to go out on maneuvers. In this way, enemy confrontations that would have caused casualties were avoided. The officers as well as all of the men in his platoon would look to him for making the decisions of where not to go. When asked, he said that he didn't believe in God at that time, and he couldn't get himself to believe that it was his intuition. He didn't know what to call this ability, despite the fact that it was always completely accurate. He knew beyond any question of doubt that this ability had saved hundreds of lives and prevented hundreds more in injuries. Sometimes it meant even overriding or not following orders from his commanding officers; yet even the officers in his platoon listened to him. In describing his state of mind, he said, "there really wasn't any mind, just instinct or something".

The mental mind had been so filled with confusion that his mentality seemed almost nonexistent, and there was a fearless clarity (little voice) that seemed to take over and tell him where to walk and where not to. He said, "it was those who were fearful, thinking about it all and dependent on their weapons rather than their minds who were the ones getting hit". When asked if he still used these abilities twenty years later, he stated, "Oh yes, for all my decisions and choices, and I still wonder about it being my intuition". He also said that this ability wasn't anything that special over in Viet Nam; there were many like him who were thrown into such chaos and confusion that the only way out alive was to call on the mind's greater abilities, even if they were not consciously aware of it being their intuition. Though we may not be living in such a life and death, or fight or flight situation, there are some messages for us in this story about fearlessness, trusting, and learning how to put the ego or intellect to one side in working with the intuition. Those of us who are developing on a elementary or even advanced level need to be persistent. We need to constantly validate our trust in ourselves and our intuitive abilities. In the section on mastery of the breath we will discuss methods for bringing into balance both the emotional and mental (ego) mind to facilitate greater ease in developing the intuition and dissolving old negative thought forms or patterns.

Creative Imagination with Emotions

All thought impulses intended for transformation into their physical equivalent, and voluntarily planted in the subconscious mind, must pass through the Imagination, and be mixed with *trust* and/or *faith*. The "mixing" of trust and/or faith with a plan, or purpose, intended for submission to the subconscious mind, may be done only through the imagination.

The subconscious mind is more susceptible to influence by impulses of thought mixed with "feeling" or emotion, than by those originating solely in the reasoning portion of the mind. In fact, there is much evidence to support the theory that only highly charged or emotional thoughts have any active influence upon the subconscious mind. It is a well known fact that emotion or feeling rules the majority of people. If this is true, than it would seem that the subconscious mind would respond more quickly to, and be influenced more readily by thought impulses which are well mixed with emotion.

It is essential to become familiar with the main types of emotions. There are basically seven major negative and seven major positive emotions. This is important to know because the negative emotions voluntarily inject themselves into the thought impulses, which insure passage into the subconscious mind. The positive emotions must be injected through the principle of auto-suggestion or affirmation, into the thought impulses which an individual wishes to pass on to their subconscious mind. All self-administered stimuli that reaches one's mind through the five senses is called self-suggestion, or auto-suggestion. Auto-suggestion is the means of communication between that part of the mind where conscious thought takes place, and that which serves as the receptor for the subconscious mind.

It is essential that we understand the method of approach to this "inner audience" of the subconscious mind. We must speak its language in order to effectively enact a positive change. The subconscious mind best understands the language of emotion or feeling. Let us now look at the seven major negative emotions, and the seven major positive emotions, so that we may draw upon and use the positives, and avoid the negatives when giving instruction to the subconscious mind. This is the prerequisite work to not only bringing about success in all aspects of the physical reality, but it is also a necessity to facilitate effective and accurate work with the intuition.

The Seven Major Negative Emotions
The emotions to be avoided are;
fear, hatred, revenge, greed, guilt, doubt, and anger.

Positive and negative emotions cannot occupy the mind at the same time. One or the other must dominate. It is your responsibility to make sure that positive emotions constitute the dominating influence of your mind. Here the law of habit will come to your aid. Form the habit of applying and using positive emotions. Eventually, they will dominate your mind so completely that the negatives will not be able to enter it. At this point you will have accomplished one of the main keys in mastery of your own life. You will effectively attract what you consciously desire into your life, and you will have also mastered one of the main building blocks for accurate use of the intuition.

The Seven Major Positive Emotions
Although there are other positive emotions, the seven major positive emotions are:
desire, love, joy, faith, enthusiasm, hope, and romance.

These are the most powerful positive emotions and are the ones most commonly used in creative effort. Work with these seven emotions (they can be mastered only through use), and the other positive emotions will be at your disposal when you need them.

Knowing effective techniques for bringing yourself to a state of balance is a necessity, for quite often it is when our emotions are a little off-center that we really need some correct or truthful answers from our Infinite. This is when it is important to know how to bring yourself to a balanced state long enough to get the needed correct answers from the intuition. If you are in a state of emotional or mental upheaval, it is suggested that you first do what you can to bring about emotional and mental stability or balance before you attempt getting answers from the Intuition. Also bear in mind that you may need to wait for a more appropriate time.

Energize Your Intuitive Mind for Creative Effort

During times of emotional-mental imbalance, you may find the following methods extremely helpful in neutralizing the imbalance. You can use methods of prayer, meditation, solitude, and being in a natural environment. You can write down the problem, or your questions, prior to going to bed so that you may access the dream state for answers. In chapter 6 you will find effective ways for balancing the mental and emotional mind through proper use of the breath. Active intuitive methods that give immediate answers (pendulums, rods, or cards) work best when an individual is in a balanced emotional and mental state. It is also true that when we are able to get accurate answers from our knowing Intuition, we will find emotional stability or calmness increased as a result.

There are many ways in which you can create an environment or setting that can help to calm the mental-emotional mind and stimulate the intuitive mind.

All stress, all tension, has the ability to shut off parts of the brain just like turning off lights in different parts of your house. When you become tense, you shut off your ability for problem solving. The more relaxed and the more positive you are, the better your brain works for you. It tunes you into both your best conscious solutions and also accurate intuitive answers. We have found the following four practices extremely helpful in offsetting the normal everyday build-up of stress and creating an environment that is conducive for stimulating the intuition.

1. **Solitude:** Go into silence, being perfectly still, and doing *absolutely nothing* for 30 minutes. This is practiced all over the world by some of the most successful, creative men and women. However, very few people in this society practice this simple method, probably due to the fast pace that most of us keep, which is the most common excuse for not taking time out.

With regular solitude practice a surge of clarity and peace within the mind will come about every time. It is a beautiful way of getting in harmony with yourself. When you feel you have the least time to do it, that is when you need to discipline yourself to do it, because usually those are the times when you need it the most. Let your mind flow without trying 30-60 minutes a day. If you have questions, write them down and sit quietly. The most appropriate answers for any questions, problems, dilemmas, or goals will come clearly and brilliantly. Sometimes we have seen it taking until the very last part of the "quiet" time for the answers to flow. Sometimes it is afterwards when you go about doing something else that the answers will flash into your mind. Do whatever it takes for you to get that quiet time. It is a necessity for your peace of mind, and a respite from the normal daily stress and tensions. If you must, go sit in your car quietly parked near a forest or a local park, with no music or any other distractions, for at least 30 minutes of absolute solitude.

2. **Deep Relaxation & Meditation:** Sit or lie down where you will be quiet, comfortable, and warm, and begin breathing deeply and completely. Begin to count down from 50 to 1, letting your mind relax during this time. Very often, in a state of calmness the answers will just flow into your mind, or immediately afterwards the flashes of insight will flow. Sometimes 10 minutes afterwards, when you begin to come conscious, a clear intuitive thought will flash into your mind, giving you the answers to your questions.

3. **Placing Yourself In a Natural Environment:** Most consciously creative individuals go for quiet walks in the woods or local parks, getting as close to a natural environment as possible. Sitting by the ocean is one of the greatest methods for stimulating creativity while listening to the powerful force of the waves pouring in. A set of cassette tapes called Environmental Series[2] which has a perfect representation of environmental sounds can also be helpful in stimulating the intuitive mind. The human being is a creature of nature and

the closer we can get back to nature in a relaxed state, the better our minds will work in all ways.

4. **Listening to Relaxing Music:** Listening to classical music such as Mozart, Bach, Beethoven, or Stravinski can be relaxing to the physical body and stimulating to the intuitive mind. Listening to this type of music can help stimulate the mind to open to ideas, insights, and the intuition. We have also found that some of what is called New Age music can be very relaxing to the mental and emotional mind, and also very stimulating to the intuitive mind.

When looking to the intuition for acquiring information or knowledge, it is helpful to know the parameters of the intuition. First comes the desire or need to know. Then comes the question or pages of questions from the conscious mind. The questions for the intuition will fall in one or more of the following categories:

1. Clear and specific goals to which you are totally committed.

2. Pressing problems which are extremely important for you to resolve.

3. Relevant questions that you ask about yourself or about another person.

4. Finding detailed information about: food, plants, animals, objects, locations, time, circumstances, and events.

To begin using any of the previously mentioned methods for problem solving, clearly define the challenging situation and write it down on paper.

Make your questions as clear and specific as possible. Utilize one of the above exercises to bring in the intuition to implement your better choice.

We recommend you go through all the research and fact-finding first, and when you have gone through all the left-brain material to compose your questions, then sit quietly using one of the above practices and allow yourself to *listen* to your own intuition. Even if all the research shows a choice in one direction, if your gut feelings or intuition tells you not to do it, then don't.

TRUST your intuition for it will always give you the answer that is best for you at that time and with that choice or situation.

---

[2] Suggested environment music for meditative listening:
Environment Series tapes 1-16, Syntonic Research Inc., New York, N.Y.
Voices of the Sea, Nature Recordings, Friday Harbor, Wa.
Lazaris and the Dolphins, Concept: Synergy, Palm Beach, Fl.

Chapter 6
MASTERY OF THE BREATH

**I Now Fully Breathe In Life,
I Relax and Trust the Process of Life.**

Mastery of the breath is one of the most beneficial skills that one can acquire in their life. The author feels this section is one of the most important parts of this entire book, for it is a way to heal all aspects of one's life. Much credit goes to Dr. Marcel Vogel for his research and formation of the basic ingredients that are contained within this section. It will be necessary to experience first-hand the dynamics of the following breath technique in order to understand its incredible power and potential.

The breath is one of the main keys for healing ourselves and for bringing about balance easily and instantly in the mental and emotional mind. When we breathe deeply, we invigorate the entire body through oxygenation of the cells, and we bring in the vital charge of energy called Prana, which is the universal lifeforce common to all forms of life. This vital force sends its currents through all systems and is absorbed down to the individual cells of the body. Your degree of health and vitality is determined by your ability to absorb and circulate prana. When you inhale deeply, you pull more prana into your body. Breathe Deep!

Mastery of the Breath

- Key to healing all aspects of the physical, mental, and emotional body.

- Bring balance of the emotional-mental mind.

- Oxygenate the cells of the body.

- Draw in Prana (universal lifeforce).

- Release the power of thought.

- Release stress. Promote relaxation.

- Neutralize negative and critical thought forms.

- Release old imprints and assist in restoring personal power.

- Release fears, doubts, anger, and resentment.

- Open psychic channels.

- Create protective psychic shields.

Prana is utilized by the mind to build the patterns of thought, being, and intention of what we wish to do, be, or perform. The act of that which we wish to do, or our intention, comes on the indwelling breath. Inhalation draws a charge into the body (negative electrical charge). Exhalation discharges an opposite polarity (positive electrical charge). Inhalation draws Prana (life force) in, and exhalation releases the power of thought. The expression of our thoughts is with exhalation. If you don't believe this, try carrying on a conversation while only inhaling.

Remember, the ego and negative emotions are the major deterrent to accessing the intuition. So, in order to successfully access the intuition, we need to remove our negative emotions, and calm our ego.

A technique for bringing about balance of the emotional and mental mind within the body can be accomplished by using the breath as the key. By imbalance we mean that which is not of a positive nature about yourself or others. To use the breath in this release method, first create the intention in your mind to be in a clear, positive, and harmonious state of mind, free from any negative or critical thoughts. Breathe in through your nose with this intention, create an image in your mind of yourself in this balanced state. Breathe out through your mouth slowly and easily, releasing any and all negative thoughts or patterns. It is best not to forcefully exhale, but ever so slowly release these negative and critical thoughts with blessings rather than with anger. Continue to breathe in through your nose, imprinting positive patterns of thoughts or affirmations towards yourself or others in the highest regard, while breathing out through your mouth any negative imprints, patterns or thoughts. Do this release and balancing exercise, breathing in and out in a connective loop; deeply, evenly, and completely. This sort of breathing technique can take up to 20 to 30 minutes to bring the body and mind to a harmonious state of clarity and balance. Again, release negative patterns of thought by breathing out through the mouth. Imprint positive patterns of thought by the breathing in through the nose.

The label Micro and Pulsed Breath were coined years ago by Marcel Vogel in his research with adept Yogi masters from India. The material that follows is a shortened version, taking a few hours of practice to start feeling the empowering affects, compared to what some masters have spent many many years in acquiring to a greater degree, of course. These invaluable breath techniques are now yours if you choose to become accomplished at them. The techniques will take practice in order to feel the full benefit and power behind them. However, once you get it, you will find many empowering ways of using them.

In the first stage in mastery of the breath, we learn how to maintain a holding pattern at the upward stroke of the indwelling breath.

Holding of the breath at the upward stroke creates what is called **Pranayama** *which opens all psychic faculties, all channels open.* As the breath is held at the upward stroke, at the peak of the inheld breath, time must be allowed for the transference of oxygen and the formation of the intent of that which you desire to do, be, or experience. As you draw in your breath to hold, you are simultaneously drawing in your clear intention or objective. Allowing some time for your intended thought to permeate the body will complete the process.

The holding of the breath at the upward stroke of the indwelling breath is **not** actually a holding of your breath in the accustomed way, but rather what is called the Micro Breath. In learning the Micro Breath, keep in mind that it is not holding the breath. It is breathing so slightly that if someone was observing you, they would think that you were not breathing at all. This is the type of breathing that the yogis do in a deep state of meditation where they appear not to be breathing and are beyond the feeling of physical pain. It is not something that takes a lifetime to learn. However, it does take some time and a good deal of practice. The first thing to learn is that in doing the Micro Breath there is no fear of not having enough oxygen. This is usually the first fear to come up and to overcome. Again, it is not a matter of holding your breath, for you will be able to maintain all body functions just fine. It is just a matter of getting use to this ever so slight breathing.

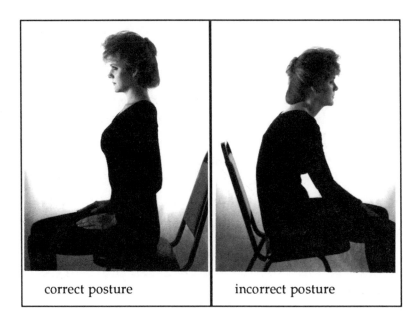

| correct posture | incorrect posture |

Micro Breath Technique:

- Sit or stand comfortably with your spine perfectly straight.

- Fill your lungs completely as you inhale.

- As you breathe in, imagine that you are drawing in with your breath large amounts of prana and circulating it through all parts of your body.

- Now, let out 1/4 of your breath and begin to maintain the Micro Breath.

- This means that your lungs will remain expanded, back straight, diaphragm in the upward position in your rib cage, rib cage completely expanded, and an ever so slight breath going in and out of your lungs slowly.

- You are not conscious of exhaling, for the air just seems to go out without noticeable movement of the lungs, and it is a sensation of drawing air in on almost a continuous basis.

- You can also sense a slight movement at the top of the lungs and sometimes a coolness in the bronchial part of the lungs. Let's now do the Micro breath again, and this time maintain it for as long as possible and feel this ever so slight in and out movement. Yet your rib cage is fully expanded while doing the Micro Breath..

Many people can maintain the Micro Breath for as long as 20 minutes, and the yogis can do this type of Micro Breath for hours. Now, try the Micro Breath again, and this time close your eyes and focus your perception from your Third eye or Ajna center, which is at the center of your forehead. What did you see? Light? When you maintain the Micro Breath your alpha brainwave greatly increases, and all of your psychic capacities or channels begin to open. Again, this state is called Pranayama, and during it one is able to see through their Ajna center, Brow Chakra or Third eye. Often, this is manifested in the ability to see light through the third eye or Brow Center. If this state is maintained long enough, you can have an out-of-body experience. The Kundalini also opens with the Micro Breath, whereby each spinal unit becomes a type of generator. The life force or prana comes in from the top of the head and with the breath goes down to the bottom of the spine in a pumping type action. When this energy hits the bottom of the spine or base, it spins up in waves in a form of a double helix (§ Caduceus).

This double helix of energy spins up and down generating an electrical field. When you draw in your breath you start the generation, and the Micro Breath with the type of holding on the indwelling breath builds the magnitude of the electrical type energy. This is what is called the raising of the Kundalini.

Pulsed Breath Technique:

The Pulsed Breath can be used for instant balancing and centering, bringing to equilibrium our mental, emotional, and physical bodies for neutralizing negative or critical thoughts or patterns. Too much positive energy such as anticipation or over excitement can equally create an imbalance, which can be balanced with the pulsed breath. The pulsed breath is the carrier wave for our thoughts and the intentions behind them. To do the pulsed breath, draw in the breath with the intention of that which you want to do. Hold the breath on the upward stroke of the indwelling breath and do the Micro Breath. Allow time for the focusing of your energy from the Heart and Brow energy centers of your body, and your intention on that which you wish to do, be, or perform. When you have reached the level of the greatest magnitude or critical mass level, the breath is quickly released through the nostrils with a strong expulsion and a snapping type contraction of the abdominal muscles and diaphragm. The Pulsed Breath is a quick release with a snorting type action of the breath through the nose. It is a snapping motion of the abdominal muscles against the diaphragm, moving upward, and forcing the air in the lungs outward through the nose with a dynamic type of snort sound. The greater the snort/snapping type action, the more power there is behind the pulsed breath to empower your intended thoughts. It takes practice to get the empowering snap of the abdominal muscles/diaphragm behind the pulsed breath to effectively cleanse, balance, or center yourself.

Practice the Pulsed Breath

Clearing and Balancing Technique: Using both the Micro and Pulse Breath.
>   Use this technique to clear negativity, bring yourself to center, and to clear the ego-intellect out of the way for intuitive questioning.

>   *To clear yourself, or if exposed to intense negative energy or feeling out of balance:*

>   Draw in the breath with your intention to clear, visualize love and light to yourself, maintain the Micro Breath, build the energy level to critical mass, and do the Pulsed Breath. Feel the instant change to balance. Now, you're ready to go about your day or to start using your tools of the intuition. Sometimes it may require doing this technique several times to neutralize any negative or critical thoughts about yourself or others.

With a clear intention, this technique will disintegrate unwanted negative or judgmental thoughts in your mind about or towards yourself or others. To be free from one's own negativity, in itself, is one of the main keys to a happy, healthy and whole life. To learn the Micro and Pulsed Breath is probably one of the most valuable skills in this entire book. We would suggest that you approach this skill with the determination to master it.

Part III
DEVELOPMENT OF THE INTUITION

Chapter 7
TOOLS FOR KNOWING YOUR INTUITIVE MIND

The tools for the intuition help individuals contact the higher aspect of themselves, their *Knowing Mind or Infinite Intelligence.* As you direct your attention more frequently to the expanded part of your brain or being, then the more frequent the expanded feelings, thoughts, sight, hearing, or touch become. The result: Your intuition develops.

There are many tools that can help you in the development of your intuition. Some tools are more effective than others. Their effectiveness depends on which one feels most comfortable to you, or which one you have greater trust in. The following tools can be used singularly or in combination to assist you in developing your intuition.

The most common internal (and more passive) tools for externalizing the intuition are prayer, meditation, creative imagination, guided visualizations, flashes, dreams, hunches or gut feelings, first impressions, and subtle sensing. External (and more active) tools include pendulums, dowsing rods, and muscle testing (Applied Biokinesiology). There are many other tools available to acquire intuitive insight into a present challenge or situation such as Rune Stones, Tarot Cards, Numerology, I Ching, and Astrology. These tools can often be very helpful in problem solving or in adding clarity to a particular situation. We don't feel that they necessarily add to the development of the intuition as a skill.

DREAMS

The subconscious mind works day and night. The process of realizing your needs and desires actually begins in the dream state. In the dream state, we work out the potential realities of our mind's own creation. We are in touch with the forces of Infinite Intelligence, even though we may be unaware of it. As we are in deep sleep, our minds will find the most practical way of creating the experiences that match our innermost desires. You cannot entirely control your subconscious mind, but you can voluntarily give it any plan, desire, or purpose which you want to transform into physical reality.

Dreams, quite simply, are a natural doorway to the inner dimensions of the subconscious mind. We usually remember very little of these deeper journeys because they reach into dimensions of experience that are quite different from the physical world as we know it. Sometimes the dreams we remember are our own attempts to translate this inner dimensional wisdom into a physical form that we can understand. In the dream world, we often feel that we are in contact with our own past and/ or future. In other words, through our dreams we communicate with other parts, aspects, or time frames of our whole being. Part of this communication is comparing notes between what goes on in our conscious waking time, our conscious and unconscious fulfillment of needs, or desires, and the exchange of information between the different levels of consciousness. During our dream state, we often receive instruction or information from our subconscious intuitive mind. The degree to which we are open to such information or wisdom is the degree to which we can transfer and incorporate this learning into our daily conscious awareness.

Dreams can be used for many purposes, including problem solving, examining our beliefs, gaining insight, and understanding current life situations. Dreams are also beneficial in promoting good health, getting in touch with repressed emotions or traumatic experiences from the past, and in making the correct decisions or choices on a daily basis. In order to take full advantage of this resource, it is important to give our dreams the proper attention they deserve.

The dream self can be just as valid as our conscious physical self. The dreaming self and the waking self are intimately connected. They are on a continuum of being and are not really separate from each other. The communication between these two parts of us continues, even when we are awake in the normal physical world. With a little practice, you can learn to bring your waking consciousness with you into the sleep state and thus merge with your "dreaming self," increasing the flow of information between the conscious and the subconscious mind.

The world of our dreams is often considered a figment of our imaginations, and is consequently considered unreal or invalid. To begin the development of this part of your being, start by looking at your dream state as a pathway of utmost importance, a pathway meant to be used, a way to discover the vast dimensions of your own identity.

Dreams can provide the conscious mind with invaluable information that we can utilize, whether or not we remember our dreams. The information may show up at any point of the day as a flash of insight from the intuition. In addition, the dream state can be a part of the mechanism we use to create our physical reality. It is here that the awesome connections and logistics are worked out. It is here that you draw specific events into your life in accordance with your beliefs and in relationship with the many other people whose realities are all intertwined.

If your day-to-day focus is fearful or negative, it is likely that your dreams will reflect the same. Dreams can be used to help you out of depression by communicating an understanding of your own knowledge to yourself on a deep, emotional level. Individuals who find themselves in this predicament can greatly benefit by using the dream state for restructuring their patterns of thinking, thereby changing the tone of their physical reality on a daily basis. For example, if you were having similar types of difficulties over and over with your relationships, you could look to your dreams to not only find the cause but also to resolve and bring about a healthy change to these patterns. It could have been something traumatic which started way back in childhood between you and your mother, father, or other family members, and which had long been pushed out of the immediate memory. Dreams can be very helpful in accessing these old experiences that created your current patterns. Once the causation or origin of a pattern is understood, the process of rewriting one's past can begin. Rewriting one's past experiences can effect a great change in one's current reality. The process of using your dreams to access information about yourself will be discussed further in the following sections.

The flow of information between the conscious and the subconscious can be greatly enhanced by a deliberate attempt to work with your dreams. By this we mean to first develop a habit of remembering your dreams, and then to learn to interpret your dreams. Then experiment a little with controlling your dreams. This sets the stage for *lucid dreaming* (dreaming in which you realize you are in a dream). In lucid dreaming there are no strict rules, you make your own rules and go at your own pace.

Recording Your Dreams

When you make the effort required for recording your dreams, you are giving them recognition and **value**. This change in attitude will automatically create a stimulating response for communication between the conscious and subconscious mind via your dreams.

Before you can record your dreams, you obviously must be able to remember them. Some people remember their dreams as a matter of course, and others do not; however, every night we *all* dream. In any case, it is usually a simple matter of remembering your dreams by using the following suggestions.

Prior to sleep, simply affirm out loud or in your mind several times the following statements:

- I am now going to remember my dreams clearly.

- Upon awakening, I am going to remember my dreams and write them down.

- I am going to wake up right after an important dream and have total recall.

You can write down your dreams directly, or use a tape recorder and write them down at a later time. Either way, it is important to get them written down on paper so that you can refer back to them. If you do not remember to record your dreams, it diminishes your capacity to take full advantage of them. Keep a separate journal or notebook exclusively for your dreams.

- Keep your notebook or recorder within reach of where you are sleeping.

- Upon awakening from a dream, don't get out of bed. Reach for your notebook or recorder, and record the dream immediately.

- Record the dream in as much detail as possible, including how you felt at different points within the dream.

- If any insights, interpretations, or associations come to you as you are recording the dream, record them also. You may have some immediate sense that the dream is providing you with intuitive insight related to something that is going on in your physical reality.

- If you are just beginning with your recording of dreams, don't be discouraged if you remember only bits and pieces. Write down whatever you remember, no matter how minute or silly it may seem, for it will encourage your subconscious mind to continue working with you in a conscious way.

If you make dreams a priority in your life, you will have no problem remembering and recording them. As with all skills of the intuition, it takes practice, patience, and determination. The effort is well worth it.

Interpreting Your Dreams

Interpreting your dreams on a regular basis is a valuable method for obtaining inner knowledge from your infinite intelligence. It is also a way to open the communication lines or language between your conscious and subconscious mind. There are many schools of thought around dream interpretation, and we have seen how much of this work does not always apply. You are a unique individual, and what may be true for you is not necessarily true for another. The only thing you can know for sure about a particular symbol or scenario is how you feel about it or where in your body you are experiencing a sensation when you recall a particular dream experience.

We recommend that you drop any preconceived notions in regards to dream interpretation. The following methods of dream interpretations are suggestions for you to try. Find the method that works best for you.

Shortly after you have had a dream and recorded it, take the time to read over it and interpret it. If you have the time, write down your interpretation immediately after recording the dream. It you don't have the time, do the interpretation within a day or so while you still have some recall. Some dreams will be so powerful that they will be embedded in your memory. Others may be hard to recall and interpret unless you get to them within a day.

With intention and practice, you will develop accurate dream interpretation. It requires listening to the voice of your intuition, or the flow of intuitive insights which are available to each of us when we listen. Dream interpreting requires the assistance of the intuition as well as the intellect (minus the ego). Ask yourself what the dream is expressing or trying to tell you, and simply trust your answers. The more you trust your intuitive/intellectual interpretations, the more skilled you will become at understanding your dreams.

It is important that your dream interpretations not be too literal. Your dreams will often point out issues and challenges that are part of your daily life. Focus your attention on the insights that come through your thoughts as a result of the concentrated attention on the dreams. The emotions you feel during a dream will also give you important clues to the overall picture. For example, if you were frightened during the dream, this might indicate that you have been focusing on fearful thoughts about a particular issue or situation. You may feel threatened about your job situation or about your life scenario in general. If you regularly have dreams in which you are being chased or attacked, for example, this may indicate that you need work in the area of your own personal power or security in life.

One of the most influential effects on the dream state is what you exposed yourself to for the 20 minutes prior to going to sleep. For many of us, the last thing we expose our minds to is violent, fearful, or catastrophic news on a television program just prior to sleep. This will in fact, have a negative influence and be a catalyst to the content of your dreams. If you wake up in the morning feeling tired, having tossed and turned all night, and your dreams felt like World War II, think about what you exposed yourself to prior to going to sleep.

With practice, you can receive information in an extremely clear and direct fashion. Then determine whether the information that is coming through the dream state is mirroring certain conscious beliefs you have towards yourself, or knowledge from your intuition (or both). If you feel you are receiving important knowledge from a teacher, guide, or from your inner source of truth, then you need only to pay attention and value such information.

Some dreams allow you to experience emotions that you may be repressing to some degree in daily life. If this is the case, the dreams can be very therapeutic. If you find yourself crying in a dream, or experiencing extreme anger, love, or terror, this may be your way of allowing yourself to express repressed emotions. Of course, if these are specific emotions that you are repressing on a regular basis, it would be for your greatest benefit to work on these emotions, beliefs, or traumatic past experiences in a more conscious and directed way.

Directing Your Dreams

Once you start remembering and recording your dreams, you can begin to exercise influence and control on them by programming yourself before you go to sleep. You may wish to program a dream to give you specific information about a current problem or dilemma. On the other hand, you may just want a dream that will lift your spirits and allow you to awaken completely refreshed, clear minded, and energetic.

You can use your dreams for creative inspirations. You can program dreams for guidance or information about practically any topic. The potential of communing with your intuitive mind through your dream state is limitless.

The technique for influencing your dreams through preprogramming by the means of positive affirmations or auto-suggestion is simple. You simply decide what type of dream you want to have, and then come up with a suggestion that expresses the essence of the dream desired. For example:

- **I will now** have a dream that will give me great insight into the upcoming decision that I have to make...

- **I will now** have a dream that will give me great insight and understanding about my relationship with...

- **I am now** going to have fun in my dreams and wake up in a great mood.

- **I will now** have a dream that will give me complete insight about my health and how I can improve it.

- **I will now** have dreams that will help me get back in touch with my inner truths, guides, teachers, or...

Give yourself the suggestion just before going to sleep. It is best to give yourself the suggestion after your mind has quieted down and you are extremely relaxed. Say aloud or in your mind several times the intention that you wish to acquire from your unconscious mind via your dream state. It is helpful to visualize your desired program dream. Imagine the dream happening just the way you want it to happen. Visualize it in your mind as vividly as you can, repeat your suggestions to yourself for a minute or so, and allow yourself to drop off to sleep.

Creative Imagination

There are no architectural limitations to castles in the air.

The creative imagination is a major component of the intuition by which we communicate our desires and dreams. As children, most of us were discouraged from using our creative imagination. Years ago, many of us were reprimanded in school for doing what was called "day-dreaming". Unfortunately, as a result of negative reinforcement, many of us learned to stifle our "day-dreaming", or our creative imagination abilities. Fortunately, many of today's more progressive educators realize that "day-dreaming" is in fact a healthy and constructive quality to be encouraged and developed within all children as a necessary skill of the creative imagination.

As children, most of us were led to believe that what we were visualizing or creating in our minds was not real. Many of us, after hearing over and over that "It's only your Imagination," started to believe that it was *all* not real. Naturally, this allowed us to come to a conclusion that anything coming from our imagination or creative faculty is probably not real. As a result, many of us ended up shutting down this faculty, the same faculty that as children filled us with wonder and awe. Perhaps when we were children we created imaginary friends. These friends could help us through traumatic or lonely times, and could also be fun and entertaining. Such an experience seems simply to be creative imagination providing us with entertainment, wonder, wisdom, and understanding from the intuitive part of our mind. For example, a case comes to mind of a woman who, as a child, created in her imagination little people or imaginary friends who were very real. These little people helped her through traumatic and lonely times in her life. They were not only there in a fun and entertaining way, but they also created experiences in a way that filled her with the wonderment of life. Recalling her childhood with the little people, she remembered how there were times of hardship when the little people were there to provide a sense of wisdom and understanding that helped her through these traumas. By the age of twenty five, the little people had become a vague memory with a feeling that it all had been unreal. We feel that the reality of this experience for this woman was a direct communication with her creative imagination that was helpful not only in providing entertainment and wonderment, but also wisdom and understanding from the intuition. This scenario may sound similar to what many of you may have experienced as children.

The faculty of creative imagination is also a part of the intuition. It is also a direct link between the finite mind of man and the Infinite Intelligence. All *so-called revelations referred to in the realm of religion, and all discoveries of basic or new principles in the field of invention, take place through the faculty of creative imagination.* It is this faculty through which "hunches" and "inspirations" are received. It is by this faculty that all bases for new ideas come into form. Through this faculty an individual may "tune in," or communicate with the subconscious minds of others, the collective consciousness of the Infinite Intelligence.

The faculty of creative imagination is one part that the majority of adults seldom use, and if they use it at all, it's by accident. A relatively small number of people use this faculty with deliberation and forethought. Those who use this faculty voluntarily, and with understanding of its functions, have the ability to operate at genius level.

The creative imagination works automatically, yet it can be stimulated in various ways as mentioned in earlier chapters. This faculty functions most often when the conscious mind is working at an exceedingly rapid rate. For example, the conscious mind can be stimulated through strong emotions such as the expression of enthusiasm, love, or sex. This form of stimulation to the conscious mind will also have a stimulating effect upon the creative imagination.

The creative imagination becomes more alert and receptive to factors originating outside the individual's subconscious mind. By this we mean that the more the individual relies upon this faculty and makes demands upon it for thought impulses, the more this faculty becomes cultivated and developed. We can cultivate and develop the creative imagination only through use. The great artists, writers, musicians, and poets became great because they acquired the habit of relying upon the "still, small voice" which speaks from within the creative imagination. It is well known to people who have "keen" imagination that their best ideas came through the so-called "hunches".

The imagination is the workshop of the mind where all ideas are fashioned and created into plans. It begins with an impulse or desire, which is then transformed into a given shape, form, or action through the aid of the imaginative faculty of the mind.

It has been said that, *"man can create anything which he can imagine."*

Our only limitation, within reason, lies in our development and use of our imagination. Some of us have not reached the apex of our development in the use of the imagination. We have merely discovered that we have an imagination and have commenced to use it in a elementary way.

Synthetic/Creative Imagination

There are two levels of the imagination. One is from the conscious mind, and the other is from the subconscious or intuitive mind. The conscious rational mind can only work through Synthetic Imagination.

The Synthetic Imagination is often used by inventors. It is the ability to arrange old concepts, ideas, or plans into a new combination, and create nothing, merely working with the material of experiences, education, and observation. The Synthetic Imagination, in conjunction with creative imagination, is needed because information gleaned from our experiences and reasoning capacities are often inadequate. However, ideas received through the creative imagination are more reliable because they come from our Infinite Intelligence, a more reputable source than what is available to the reasoning faculty of our mind. An example of an inventor using both forms of the imagination follows: A scientific invention is begun by organizing and combining known ideas, or principles accumulated through experiences, through the synthetic faculty (the reasoning left brain). If this accumulated knowledge is found to be insufficient for the completion of the invention, the source of knowledge available is then drawn upon via the creative faculty, or infinite intelligence. The procedure will vary from individual to individual, but it will nonetheless remain in relative order;

1. They stimulate their mind so it functions on a higher-than-average plane, usually through single-minded focus backed with great desire or enthusiasm (emotion).

2. They concentrate upon the known factors (the finished part) of the invention, and create in their mind a perfect picture allowing the subconscious mind to take over. They relax by clearing all thoughts from their minds, and then waiting for the answer to "flash" into their brains.

Sometimes the results are both definite and immediate. At other times, the results may be negative, depending upon the state of development of the intuitive creative faculty, and the state of mind (whether it was positive or negative) prior to the onset of the task.

Both the synthetic and creative faculties of imagination become more alert with use, just as any muscle or organ of the body develops through use. Your imaginative faculty may have become weak through inaction, but it can be revived and made alert through use. Center your attention on the development of your creative imagination.

Consciously Using Your Creative Imagination

The creative imagination can be stimulated by visualizing, or guided imagery. To develop this aspect of your intuition, spend time on a daily basis focusing on or visualizing your projects from work or in your home. These projects can be as tangible as something you are making, to goals in your life such as financial, physical, emotional, mental or spiritual. As in some of the techniques in chapter 5, spend 30 minutes each day (preferably early morning) to visualize the complete picture of your goal or project. Visualize it completely in as much detail as you can create. Use as many of your senses as possible in this creation. For example, "What is its shape, size, color?", or "Does it have a smell, light, sound to it? ", and most of all, "What does it feel like, or what emotions are involved?" See if there is a difference between visualizing with your eyes open or closed. Some people visualize best with their eyes open as with day-dreaming. Sometimes defocusing of the eyes can be helpful in starting the process.

Creative Imagination Technique

- Find a quiet area to sit for 30 minutes, free from distraction, that is environmentally conducive or stimulating for creative visualization. This technique works best during your first hour in the morning.

- First see your goal or project in its completed form with as much detail as possible. Of course this may change a little as time goes on while working through the details.

- Now start working on the details. It helps to break the big picture down to workable sections.

- Begin working on the individual parts, seeing every aspect, every detail. It is here that you can create, build on, delete, or do further problem solving. At this stage allow the mind to be free from all logic or limitations. There is an adage that says, "There are no architectural limitations to sand castles in the air." In other words, allow all thoughts, all ideas, all possibilities to flow through. Be open to your intuitive impressions.

- When your 30 minutes are up, start writing everything that came across your mind as fast as possible with as much detail as possible. No matter how inconsequential or silly the thought may be, write it down. Keep a journal of this information. What you may think is not important now may be so weeks or months down the line.

- Repeat this exercise daily at the same time, and you will find the quality of the results will increase.

This exercise can save you a great deal of trial-and-error. The time used for doing this technique will save you three times or more effort in obtaining your perfected end product or goal. The greater detail and the more emotion you can include with your focused imagery, the less time it will take to bring your goals into reality.

Secrets of Effective Prayer

Often you will notice that most people will resort to prayer only after everything else has failed. Most people pray as a ritual of meaningless words. When people only pray after everything else has failed, they go to prayer with their mind full of fear and doubt, which are emotions that the subconscious mind acts upon, and passes on to the Infinite Intelligence. Consequently, the Infinite Intelligence receives that fear and doubt and then acts upon them accordingly. I recall going through horrendous emotional growth pains in my early twenties, when I prayed for strength because seemingly nothing else worked. I asked continually for strength and would in turn create for myself an unpleasant experience where I would have to rely on greater strength to make it through the situation. It seemed, every time a cry for help went out through prayer, Bam!, there was another hard, painful experience to go through. It didn't take a fool to figure it out. Be careful of not only what you ask for, but also how you ask for it. I realized then how the etheric level works: *Like Attracts Like*.

If you pray for something, but you fear that you may not receive it, or if you fear that your prayer will not be acted upon, then your prayer will have been in vain.

Prayer can result in the realization of what the prayer was all about. If you have received what you prayed for, go back in your memory, recall your state of mind while you were praying, and record that state of mind, the emotion, and the content of the prayer. Keep this positive memory to reinforce the effective power of prayer. You may recall that the effective prayers included a positive affirmative state of mind filled with strong positive emotions, like love, desire, and enthusiasm.

The subconscious mind is the intermediary, which translates your prayers into terms that the Infinite Intelligence can recognize. It presents the message and brings back the answer in the form of a definite plan or idea for bringing the object of the prayer into reality. This is why sometimes mere words read from a prayer book cannot always serve as an agency of communication between your conscious mind and your Intuitive or Infinite Intelligence. In other words, it is using positive affirmative statements backed by strong positive emotions that create a winning combination for effective prayer.

If you are using prayer for acquiring answers from the Infinite Intelligence or God (however you may perceive him/her/them to be), then you may find the experience a little disappointing. There are two old adages which we would like to share with you: "God gave us two ears and one mouth, which should be used proportionately", and, "Prayer is talking to God, and Meditation is listening to God". In order to develop the ability to listen to the subtle answers of your prayers, you may find one of the methods in chapter 5 helpful in creating an environment conducive to effective prayer.

Three Steps Beyond With Subtle Sensing

There are three types of Subtle Sensing: Clairvoyance, Clairaudience, and Clairsentience. Most of us, if not all of us, have experienced subtle sensing to various levels and degrees.

Clairvoyance (sight): Is the ability to have visions or expanded sight. For some, this means having complete imagery of a particular event, problem solving, or visual experience. For others it may involve seeing split second symbols, or the energy around all life forms. When individuals have these types of visual imagery, the symbols usually have feeling with them and they move very fast. Before an individual has a chance to analyze these symbols, the subconscious is on to another and then it's gone again. In other words, the symbols may be fleeting leaving the individual with an overview interpretation. With the symbols, one can be left with a deep knowing or understanding mixed with a feeling or emotion.

Clairaudience (hearing): Is the ability to hear words or clear and concise audible communications in your mind. It usually seems like it is coming from outside of you, yet there will be no one around you. The communications usually don't seem like the normal voice of your mind. Sometimes, it will be the voice of a loved one or of someone very familiar. Usually, though, it is your own inner voice that sounds very different from your normal everyday communication of your thinking mind. Out of the three categories of subtle sensing, it is the most difficult to distinguish between one's own inner communications and the daily mind stuff. On the other hand, clairaudience can be very definite, very impulsive, and dynamic. Sometimes clairaudience can even be insistent, where you *Know* what to do, and it means doing it right now.

Clairsentience (feeling): includes first impressions or spontaneous inclination, hunches or gut feelings, intuitive flashes, or actively feeling energy. Clairsentience refers to a heightened state of feeling. Usually this state is more valid or reliable, for one's feelings very rarely lie. When you begin to put your feelings out to the world: What's going on? How does this feel? Is it balanced? Constructive? Positive? You will get very definite messages back. Clairsentience is the most widely used form of subtle sensing and it is the easiest to develop.

Subtle sensing does not always mean information recognized by the cognitive processes of the brain. Clairsentience also refers to the ability to sense other people's emotions, which is called empathy. It is an experience where the subtle feelings seem like something that you would feel within yourself. Some people do not recognize the emotions they pick up from others though their own body. In other words, our bodies often react to the emotional states of others. This physical response can sometimes be felt as tension in the neck or shoulders, a tightening or nausea in the abdomen area. The thoughts that may accompany these feelings may be "I don't know why I feel this way," "I don't normally feel like this," "I feel so depressed since talking to ___and I don't know why," "I feel so tired being around ___." These sort of statements could be the result of someone else's moods (critical or negative thoughts) or wishes. It is usually the negative, critical, or judgmental thoughts of others that can have such an adverse effect upon your conscious being. The object here is to recognize the imbalanced emotions and to understand when the source is outside of yourself. To neutralize such negative effects from other's emotions, see chapter 6 on using the breath for clearing and balancing. Knowing the difference between your own and another's emotional thoughts or needs can be helpful to consciously "tune out" unwanted emotional stimuli. Knowing when and when not to be open is very important to keep in mind as you grow with your development of the intuition.

First Impressions

First impressions are one of the basic forms of our intuitive capacities or subtle sensing. These first impressions are correct 100% of the time. You probably remember when doing multiple choice question tests taking in school, that your first choice answers were usually the correct ones. In test situations like that, you may also remember how doubt took over in your mind and you changed the answers, finding out later that your first choice was in fact correct. This has been observed hundreds of times in classroom situations, and is considered by educators a standard guideline. The author has seen this to be true at his gem and crystal store, where the customer, upon entering the store, will be drawn immediately to a particular crystal by sight, sound, or feel, and will proceed to walk around the store picking up twenty to thirty other pieces, only to return to the piece that they were originally drawn to. This first impression is a form of communication from your intuition and if **listened** and **responded** to immediately, will develop into a intuitive tool that you can use accurately on a regular basis for making choices and decisions.

Intuitive experiences come in many forms. The first key in the development of the intuition, as we have said, is **subtle listening**. Listen to those "first thoughts" or feelings, that we sometimes call spontaneous inclinations, gut feelings, hunches, or simply the "knowing" feelings. Often-times, first impressions occur in a fraction of a second, and are so fast that to our conscious thought they may not get a chance to be acknowledged before a conscious judgement is made by the ego-intellect. These first impressions are not necessarily lost, but sometimes obscured from the conscious mind. They have been recorded in their original form within the subconscious. This is mainly applicable with material things that we have misplaced, or with people we may judge based on appearances or social conditioning. This, once again, is an example of conditions where the ego-intellect can have an effect on a first impression or conscious intuitive thought before it can be acknowledged and registered.

Those people who are aware of their intuitive abilities are typically attuned to their expanded senses, clairvoyance (sight), clairaudience (hearing), and clairsentience (feeling). By using various external tools such as pendulums, dowsing rods, or cards, the intuition can be externalized and developed as well. The use of these tools can be extremely helpful in accessing specific quantitative and qualitative answers from the intuition which will be discussed in the following chapter. The expanded ability of feeling or clairsentience is used in both passive intuitive work as with first impressions, prayer, dreams, hunches, and actively as with the external tools of the intuition.

Beyond Your Feeling Hands

The ability to feel subtle energies through your hands or various other parts of your body is referred to as clairsentience. The experience of the subtle energies can be sensed as a feeling of vibration, tingling, warmth, or coolness. For most people, the left hand is the receiving hand, and the right hand is the projection hand. In other words, for most people, the left side of the body emits a more receptive and magnetic type of energy that is feminine in nature. The right side of the body, which is controlled by the left brain, emits a projecting and electrical type of energy that is masculine in nature, and can be used for projecting out energy. For most people, the left hand can be used for sensing the difference between two or more objects, such as foods, vitamins, remedies, crystals, or for finding the right answer with a Yes/No technique (3-card method) that will be discussed later. Whether you are a dominant right or left-handed person may have a bearing on whether you sense (feel) with your right or left hand. If you are in question as to which hand you sense with, try both and feel which one gives you the greatest results. Subtle sensing with your receiving hand will be felt in the form of a tingling, warmth, vibration, or in some cases a coolness. Another example of subtle sensing is when a person feels such an affinity with the object they are holding in their hand that they don't want to put it down. We have seen many people pick up such objects as quartz crystals that they felt an affinity for and they just can't seem to put that particular piece down because it feels glued to their hand. This is another way for the body to subtly communicate a rapport, harmony, or attraction with an object.

To physically and energetically feel the vibrational field or the energy frequencies of an object requires some development of your ability to subtle sense with your hands.

This ability can be developed with the following exercise. This exercise will also stimulate the minor energy chakras (vortices) in your hands.

- First of all, draw in your breath and begin to do the Micro breath, which will open all of your psychic channels.

- Begin to rub the palms of your hands together briskly for one minute while maintaining the Micro Breath. One minute of rubbing your hands together will feel like a long time. Meanwhile you are generating a great deal of heat in your hands, and you are also allowing the Micro Breath to help you integrate your intention while all of your psychic faculties are beginning to open.

- Then sensitize your hands by opening them with palms side by side facing up, and ever so lightly blow on your open hands.

This experience will give you a reference point, for you will feel one or more of the following sensations: vibration, tingling, warmth, coolness, or a sensation

*of light or sound that may even be felt in other parts
of your body. You may also have sensed a bright
light in your mind at the brow chakra area.*

After doing this subtle sensing warm up, experiment
by running your hand over selected objects such as a
quartz crystal, a plant, or various pieces of gemstone
jewelry of gold or silver with your hand at a distance of
not more than four inches away from the object. Make
notes of the differences between the objects. Did they
feel cold, warm, vibrating, evoke an emotion, or a sense
of light, color, etc.? With practice you will feel different
types of sensations from different objects. When you
have accomplished this beginning level of subtle sensing
by feeling the vibration or sensation of the energy field
around the object, try pulling your hand slowly further
and further away from the object until you can no longer
feel the vibrational field. Note at what distance you can
still feel the sensation of the object. Your mind should
still be quiet and your attention completely focused as
you do this. How far does the energy field extend from
the object? The distance at which you can feel the object
indicates either the vibrancy of the lifeforce within the
object or to what degree you resonate with the object.
Maintaining the Micro Breath throughout the exercise
will help immensely in keeping yourself centered and
focused, which means keeping the rational, thinking mind
quiet (see Chapter 6 on Micro Breath).

Some people are able to immediately feel the energy
emanating from the different objects. Others need more
time in development. If you don't experience the
sensations the first time, do it again and again, doing it
several times a day, every day, until you succeed. It will

take time and practice. You will eventually feel the vibrations of these objects.

This exercise not only develops the sensitivity of the hands but it also stimulates the thyroid and parathyroid glands to secrete hormones that result in energy being sent into the upper centers of the head. This in turn will cause the pituitary gland to be stimulated, thereby opening and increasing the intuitive capacities. The heart will also be energized, and the mind will have greater clarity that allows for greater concentration. This exercise is a lesson not only about subtle sensing with the hands, but also about listening or fine-tuning with the mind. If you experience difficulty with this, it is only because that part of the brain and sensory equipment may be a little out of practice. Also, keep in mind that many of us sense these energies in different ways, so it is suggested that you try the exercise with variation as to which hand you use, time of day, and location.

Feeling with your receiving hand can be used for selecting the right foods, vitamins, crystals or other objects. The feeling of a vibration, tingling, warmth, or other type of sensation works best when you incorporate it with your questioning to your intuitive mind. You can also use this ability to sense with your hand imbalances within the body of an animal or another human being. It can be a very accurate detector of abnormalities, dysfunctions, or disorders within your body or within others.

The ability to feel the energy is not only a matter of building the sensitivity of the hands, but also of strengthening the mental focus. In order to achieve the focus you need, you first must become still in your mind and body. If you find your mind is wandering, drop your attention for a moment and then gently return your attention to your sensing hand while maintaining the Micro Breath.

As you work on developing the sensitivity of your hands and the concentration of your mind, your intuitive abilities will begin to increase. The more you use your intuitive abilities, the less your intellectual mind will be involved. As you develop your intuitive abilities, you may find yourself relying on these other ways of knowing for they will naturally seem to open up for you. Your subtle sensing abilities will develop as you physically or energetically feel more of the subtle energies that surround all objects and life forms. As this develops, your mind will not question your ability to know something without knowing how you knew it. This type of sensing will not seem to be based on any intellectual reasoning, but nonetheless, you will be able to confirm the accuracy at a later time. Learn to trust and rely on this sensing. The experiences will, in turn, reinforce and build the accuracy of your intuitive sensing. This does not mean that you ignore the information coming in from your physical reality. In fact, it is best that you use the information from your physical reality to test the accuracy of your intuitive sensing. Again, the important thing is to first acknowledge your intuitive experiences, then to trust them, and finally to respond to them.

It is advisable to cross-reference the results acquired from the use of intuitional tools such as hunches, pendulums, dowsing rods, and muscle testing with the following subtle sensing technique. The following subtle sensing technique can be used to answer Yes and No type questions, or it can be used as a means to verify other intuitive questioning.

Three Card Subtle Sensing Technique:

In this technique we use the subtle sensing of our left hand (for most of us), and the Micro Breath.

- Take three clean small pieces of heavy blank white paper, fold each one in half. Write on the inside of one Yes, one with No, and leave one blank.

- Fold them, thoroughly shuffle them together, and lay them on the table about 2-3" inches apart.

- Now, state what you feel is intuitively true about the subject in question, or to verify the results of other forms of intuitive questioning. Your statement of question could be something like: "Infinite Intelligence, I would now like verification or clarification that the preceding information is totally accurate and true at this time."

• Draw in your breath with your intention and maintain the Micro Breath, while you place your cupped left hand, palm down, over each card on the table without touching them, and feel the cards one by one; go back and forth until you feel a distinctive difference in your hand with either a tingling, warmth, or vibration. If nothing happens, try it again or at another time. If you get a blank card, this means either maybe, greater or lesser degrees, or rephrase the question/s. The blank or maybe answer could really mean maybe or to go back to your original intuitive questioning and check again to see if the answers are totally accurate. The intuition can be very demanding for total accuracy. Sometimes the real answer depending on perspective, is neither Yes or No. It takes some time getting used to the communication or the perspective of your intuition. If it is a Yes answer, then most likely you can add a great deal more validity to your original intuitive answers. By using this technique, we have found errors in the precision of our questions and answers, and sometimes we have found extraneous variables that were not taken into account.

You can learn more from your line of questions that come into your conscious mind than you can from the answers you receive.

Chapter 8
THE SCIENCE & ART OF THE PENDULUM

Tools for the intuition such as pendulums and dowsing rods go back to 8000 B.C., and were used by the Hebrews, Egyptians, Chinese, Romans, Greeks, Druids, Hindus, Peruvians, and the American Indians. Even Moses was a skilled dowser. In the Bible there are several references to Moses being a water wizard, meaning that he was able to find water with a dowsing staff. The Egyptians also used dowsing rods and pendulums, not only for finding water and gold, but also for divination. The Chinese would call for a Radiesthesist, a person adept at using a pendulum or other tool for sensing the unseen energies around potential building sites, to detect, as they would have said, "The Claw of the Dragon." "The Claw" probably corresponds to what we now call the harmful rays of a positive-charge vortex or positive-charge ley lines.

The scientific use of a pendulum is called *Radiesthesia* which means the detecting and measuring of an entire spectrum of radiations whether mineral, plant, animal, or human. There is no magic in Radiesthesia. Most people have this faculty. It consists of the ability to receive rays of light or waves of sound that surround all of us, and all objects. These waves or vibrations are then passed on through the muscular reflexes to the instrument that is being used, such as the pendulum or dowsing rods. Some people will be more proficient at this than other people. Dowsing, on the other hand, usually refers just to the search for water or minerals. Both the pendulum and dowsing rods are direct communication devices between the conscious and subconscious mind as a way to externalize the intuition. It is a matter of establishing the language between the two parts of the brain. We can draw an analogy between a computer and our brain to underscore the relationship between the conscious, the subconscious, and the tools of the intuition. In this analogy, the brain would be likened to the greatest computer hardware, the pendulum and dowsing rods are the interface between the conscious and subconscious, and the applications are the techniques or software which put us in the position of effectively using our greater intuitive capacities.

The Pendulum

The pendulum is one of the oldest tools of the intuition still in wide use to this day. A pendulum is a small weight suspended from a chain, or string, preferably about 3-6" in length. The types of pendulums vary immensely, and the various types can have differing results. A pendulum can be made of almost any substance, however, it is recommended that it be neutral. Neutral substances include wood, glass, plastic or crystal, neutral in color, such as clear or black. By this we mean that all metals and colors have a frequency or vibration to them that could have an influence on the results of the test. For example, if you were testing for a particular substance such as a mineral and your pendulum contained that mineral or something similar to it, the presence of the substance in your pendulum being in close proximity to that which you are testing could create inaccuracy in your test results. On the other hand, this kind of result is preferred when testing for a particular substance such as gold, silver, or oil. Often, when searching for such a substance, a special type of pendulum with a screw top with a hollow inside is used. The hollow serves as a place to put samples of the material you are seeking. Further details will be discussed in later sections. We have found many objects to work well for a pendulum including lead crystal, quartz crystal, and a wooden plumb bob. Some pendulists may have twenty or more different types of pendulums for many applications. Find a pendulum that feels comfortable to you. It's purpose is to assist you in externalizing your intuition. It is not the source of your answers.

Your Approach to the Pendulum
Your approach to effective and accurate testing with a pendulum requires:

- Your mind be in a neutral, quiet, questioning state, never letting thought or desire interfere with or influence the answers you seek.

- It is important to keep an "I don't know" attitude. If a condition was negative yesterday, I really don't know about it today; it may be the same, it may have improved or regressed.

- You must be aware of what your mind is doing at the time of the questioning. Any thoughts about a possible answer, any personal desire, and any ego involvement or tendency to show off will influence your work.

- If you are centered and balanced, and your questions are completely objective, you can trust the answers.

After you have worked with the pendulum for a while you will gain confidence. Start with some simple exercises, and move on to more complex work. However, when doing personal questioning and you have an investment in the outcome such as personal or capital gain, we strongly suggest that you see the answers as, "Oh, this is very interesting, but, we'll see." If you see the same answers coming up over and over, month after month, then there may be greater validity to the acquired answers.

Approach the pendulum with *enthusiasm* and with *confidence* that you are able to do it, for a half-hearted or doubtful attitude will only result in uncertain findings. Always work in quiet surroundings by yourself if at all possible, away from sceptics, negative thoughts, or anyone trying to influence you. Seeing yourself, the operator, as a super-sensitive receiver will help in your development.

When doing your pendulum work, find a quiet area with a minimum of electrical or metal objects around you. You may support your elbow on the table or hold your elbow tucked close to your waist in order to override certain controlling muscles that can have a biasing effect on results. Always avoid crossing or touching your hands or feet during the test, for you could short circuit yourself and disrupt the accuracy of your flow of information.

To begin using the pendulum, first hold the string or chain in your dominant hand. Hold the string of the pendulum between your thumb and forefinger with your wrist slightly arched (usually with the right hand), so that the pendulum can have a direct drop. Extend and separate the last three fingers of your pendulum hand so that the fingers do not touch each other. This allows the extended fingers to act as a sort of antennae. Feel if this is comfortable for you. For some people, using the opposite or left hand may be more effective. Experiment with both hands until you find which hand is more comfortable or works more effectively for you. The pendulum can now move easily back and forth or side to side.

Pendulum Language

Basic identifying means setting up the language between your conscious mind, sub-conscious mind or intuition, the energetics of the body, and the subtle muscle movement of the hand and fingers that will cause the pendulum to move. The language is comprised of five directions; forward and backwards, side to side, clockwise and counter-clockwise, or no movement. Establishing the direction of your pendulum language is as simple as drawing a six-inch circle on a piece of paper with a crisscross in the center, dividing the circle into four sections. Give the pendulum a 3-6" inch length on the string and hold directly over the cross on the **Pendulum Language Chart***, or your circle drawn on a piece of paper. Look at the chart, remove your attention from the pendulum; focus the intention with your mind to establish the pendulum language.

Pendulum Language Chart

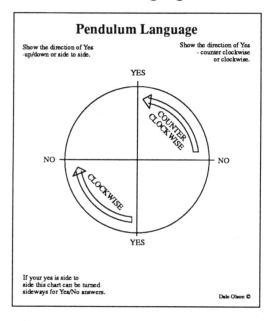

Knowing Your Intuitive Mind: Pendulum Charts
D. W. Olson, Crystalline Publishing, Eugene, OR

It helps to speak the intentions out loud. Being precise, specific, positive, and affirmative with the communication to your subconscious mind is absolutely imperative for success and accurate results. For example, "Intuitive mind, please indicate the direction of **Yes** for me." For most people this can be indicated by either a backwards and forwards swing, or a right-handed or clockwise gyration. For most people a side-to-side swing, or a counter-clockwise direction indicates a **No** answer. A swing that is in between can indicate more-or-less, maybe, or rephrase the question. Now, with your mind, direct your pendulum into action by making your statement; "Intuition, or Infinite Intelligence, now indicate to me which direction is Yes." Then, find the direction for No,

Maybe, and so on. If you are left-handed try the pendulum in the left hand, for that may work best for you. If there is little movement, relax, breathe in and out several times and try again. Again, verbally state your request, "show me which direction is Yes with large swings." Sometimes patience is needed for the communication to become established, and for some people the pendulum responds immediately. If there is a problem with making it move, perhaps it is a matter of too much focus on the pendulum which means there is too much attention of the mental or emotional mind involved in trying to make it work. Most often, success requires a defocusing of the mental and emotional mind. This defocusing can be achieved by holding your arm tucked against your waist to one side of your body, wrist arched with pendulum hanging freely so that the pendulum is seen more out of your peripheral vision than by direct sight.

If you state a question and the pendulum does not move at all, it may mean that:

1. there may be a more appropriate time and place for the questioning,

2. there may be a more appropriate way to state the question, or

3. wait for a better state of mind.

Timing, place, and emotional-mental balance are the most important variables to be considered. Always ask, "Is this the right time and/or the right place to be asking this question?" Or, "Should I rephrase the question?" If NO, then wait for another time or place, or go on to another question. By asking the questions, "Is this the right time, place, or appropriate question?", you are able to establish trust and respect with your intuition.

If you should get slow answers, it can be helpful to cup your hands around running water, or place a natural quartz crystal in your hand for 5 minutes or more. This will help you to increase your energetic level to facilitate more effective pendulum work. With pendulum work, it is usually the intuition, subconscious mind, and an unconscious slight muscular movement that causes the pendulum to move. However, when first beginning, it may be helpful to artificially overcome inertia by giving the pendulum a slight motion, then let the natural force take over the motion. If you have difficulty in making the pendulum move or in being consistent, then consider: Are you tired, forcing the situation, or in an imbalanced state? If so, give it a rest and approach it at another time.

Once you have established the communication with your intuition, you can begin your development by working with questions to which you already know the answers. With practice, you will acquire a feel for the pendulum, and we would suggest that you do not go on to more advanced questions until you consistently get accurate results to questions you already know the answers to. This enables you to establish a consistent language with your intuition. It takes time and patience to develop these abilities because it takes time for the subconscious mind to tune into the information requested and for the different parts of your being to become familiar with the language of the pendulum and the various aspects of your own consciousness.

It is also very helpful to keep a journal of your work to record the questions asked, how they were asked, time of day, where you did your pendulum work, direction you were facing, and most importantly, to keep track of the accuracy of both your hits and misses.

Pendulum Language with checking objects

As you become more proficient with the pendulum and the language between your conscious and subconscious mind, you will find a system that works for you. Whenever you hold the pendulum over any object, animate or inanimate, you will pick up the radiations from it and the pendulum will usually begin to oscillate. Most often, the pendulum will first swing away from you and then back towards you. This signifies the neutral swing, which merely puts you in contact with the object. As soon as you ask a question the pendulum will answer by rotating. For most people, if it rotates to the right or clockwise, it is saying "**Yes**"; this is the positive swing, indicating a positive or harmonious condition. If it rotates to the left, counterclockwise, it is usually saying "**No**"; which is a negative swing, indicating a negative or inharmonious condition. The degree to which the pendulum rotates will indicate the extent of your answer. If you ask a question which does not have a yes or no answer, and is confused, or if it doesn't have an answer, then the pendulum will oscillate side to side indicating a **No** answer. You may have made a mistake in how you asked the question; try rephrasing your question.

Repeat the test on establishing your pendulum language a few times a day for at least a week to make sure your answers are consistent. This will help to establish the programming of the language with the subconscious mind, for the subconscious mind must fully understand what is expected of it for proper communication to take place. In the beginning it is best to practice for short periods, 20 minutes or less. As the strength of your energy increases, so can the duration of your testing increase.

Effective Pendulum Use

It is good practice to preface your intuitive work with an affirmation or prayer such as "Open the way for that which is for the highest and greatest benefit," or "Let this be of Thy will and not my will," or "I invoke the Christ within, I am a clear and perfect channel, Love and Light is my guide." Find an affirmation or prayer that works for you and your belief system. *Affirmations and/or prayer will help to offset the interference of the ego or the intellect.*

In training your intuitive capacities, it is important to check your results for accuracy, to be honest with yourself, and to **TRUST your "inner voice"**. Instead of being afraid to be "wrong", practice again and again until you are successful. Eventually you will succeed because these are natural human abilities that you have lost touch with through lack of use. Again, it is a reminder that *we learn more from our mistakes than we do from our successes, and by tuning into the tools, we learn, and experience less and less trial and error.*

It is imperative to be in a balanced state prior to using the following techniques to get accurate results with your intuition. *Fears, doubts, anger, guilt, resentments, sadness can be released* by using the Micro and Pulsed Breath. The following technique is another quick and easy way to release the negatives. Simply release these negative thoughts by inhaling deeply through the nose, focusing your intention of releasing the negative or critical thoughts and exhaling from the mouth, slowly and completely, connecting breaths, never forcing the breath out through the mouth. Continue this technique until you feel the proper balanced state of being (20-45 minutes).

There are times when a pendulum does not work accurately. Sometimes the pendulum will not respond to questions, will act sluggish, barely move, or simply hang still. Audible music will sometimes confuse the reading. Sometimes the pendulum may not be an accurate tool especially during conditions including electrical storms, earthquakes, tidal waves, volcanic eruption, or atomic testing in your area. These conditions will disturb the electromagnetic energy field of the earth. It is highly recommended that you avoid pendulum readings around full moons, solar flares, or rooms full of people for the same reason. Also, if you are very tired or ill, these are times that may be avoided. That is why it is best to always ask, "Is this the best time to do this pendulum reading/test?"

Before we discuss some of the infinite uses of the pendulum, we would like to mention another area that is best to avoid because it does not deal with facts, and that is predicting the future. If you misuse the pendulum in the way that many people have misused the Ouija board, you will be using the pendulum at the level of a parlor game. If you are trying to find out when you are going to die, whether you should marry someone, and other types of fortune-telling, it is safe to say that you may find yourself greatly disappointed. If you merely play with the pendulum as if it were a game, the results will be superficial and you will only get what is in your own subconscious mind or misinformation due to lack of appropriateness.

When used properly, the pendulum tunes into the universal consciousness where the energy of higher intelligence will bring forth the right information. Those who work at predicting the future know that the time element is the most difficult to forecast. The only time the pendulum, or subconscious can tell you something in the immediate future is when the information is already present in the human consciousness. You cannot get an accurate reading before people have made up their minds about an event or outcome. *When you work objectively, new information and facts can accurately be discovered that were previously unknown to you.*

The main keys to your success will be keeping yourself objective and detached from the outcome, and being extremely precise with your questions. *In your communications with your intuition, your answers will be only as good as your questions.* It does require certain knowledge on the subject in order to know what questions to ask. Your questioning will work best when the questions are stated in a positive format, such as:

Now is the best time to do this reading?

This is the best place to do this?

My intuitive accuracy is what % today?

It is to my highest and greatest benefit to _____ at this time, at what %__?

This plant is in need of_____?

The lost object is what direction or degree from this point?

This body is in need of what remedy for this situation?

For this person's highest and greatest benefit, their need is?

It is also very helpful to keep an accurate log or journal of your results to help you keep track of your improvement in accuracy. When you have completed your pendulum session, it is helpful to give thanks to your intuition and Infinite Intelligence for being of service, for those parts of your being appreciate the acknowledgment, and most likely will be more apt to assist you in the future.

Ways to Use the Pendulum

There are basically four ways in which to use the pendulum:

1. The pendulum is held directly over an object or body and the questions are asked concerning this object or body.

2. The pendulum is held over an object like food or a remedy which is being held in your left hand and questions asked regarding the object's relationship to yourself, or another.

3. A screw top sample pendulum is used to dowse for a like substance. The substance is placed inside the pendulum as a sample (Witness Method).

4. The "Witness Method" makes it possible to work on testing objects, substances, or measuring variables for yourself or someone else by means of samples of maps, photos, and or Pendulum Charts. See Pendulum Applications for further details.

Now that you have established your pendulum language directions and have the parameters of the do's and don'ts, lets do some testing of the pendulum and yourself. First, hold your pendulum over the top of your left hand; if working properly, the top of your left hand will cause the pendulum to gyrate in a clockwise motion indicating a positive energy. Now turn your hand over, palm up and check; this should cause the pendulum to gyrate in a counter-clockwise motion, indicating a negative receptive energy. You will experience the opposite findings if using your left hand with the pendulum and your right hand for the test.

The second test is for *accuracy*. This is done by checking separate papers with mathematical calculations, some correct and some with errors. Mix them up, place them face down on a table, and find the correct ones through positive readings and the incorrect ones by negative readings. This can be a helpful test, however, we find that our abilities work best when we have a good reason for working with the object being tested. The intuition itself does not like to be tested. If you are trying to trick the intuition or question its validity, then you will most likely get inaccurate answers for it is an indication of lack of trust and your answers will reflect this. These tests are a matter of developing accurate communication lines. Trust needs to be formed before you start. Of course, the more proof of your accuracy the deeper and stronger will be your trust in your intuitive abilities. Having a level of 80% or greater accuracy is definitely an accomplishment. In other words, it is okay to be less than 100% accurate with the development of your intuition. Just remind yourself of your successes. This is the main purpose of keeping a journal.

The third test is a *sensitivity* test. This is a good test to do at various times under various conditions. Stand erect, facing due West, relax as much as possible, place your left hand directly over your solar plexus, palm inward with the fingers closed. Suspend the pendulum from the right hand, using the full length of the string, so that the pendulum is opposite the center of the top of the left hand and about 8" inches out from the left hand. The pendulum will start to gyrate in a clockwise direction. Count the number of gyrations carefully, and if the gyrations are weak and less than fifteen, your chances of getting any reliable results are remote. Try another time or place. The degree of sensitivity and strength is indicated by the number of gyrations, and although they vary considerably from individual to individual, they can be grouped roughly as follows: 15-30 weak, 30-50 medium, and 50-100 good. These figures represent the number of complete gyrations and not gyrations per minute. This is an interesting test, for it indicates that the human body is extremely sensitive to outside influences, and can be measured accordingly.

Pendulum Applications

It is helpful to remind yourself from time to time that it is not the pendulum or the rods that are giving the answers. They are simply practical tools to externalize the intuition. It is your inner higher intelligence, communicating through the nervous system, which gives you the signals. The pendulum moves as a result of the nerve and muscle response to the signal from the intuition. The conscious mind interprets the meaning of the signals through codes set up between your conscious and subconscious mind. A good dowser or pendulum operator does not just see the answers in the movement of the rods or pendulum, they also feel or sense the answers in terms of frequency registrations in their hand, arm, or entire body. Most often this comes after persistent training and development. It does help to defocus from the pendulum or rods to help keep the intellect out of the way, and in this defocusing process one is able to step into an altered state of consciousness, which is the higher aspects of the intuition.

We can use pendulums and dowsing rods to assist us in many ways. We can choose the right foods, diet, vitamins, minerals, supplements, crystals, books, remedies, jobs, locations, cars, and relationships We can use these tools to help us **choose** careers, teachers, doctors, employees, locations to live, or the right house. Pendulums can be instrumental in helping us **find** things: the right job, lost objects, missing people, buried treasure, underground water and electrical lines, water, minerals, metals, or oil. We can use them to **discover** the relationship compatibility of partners and friends, personal motivators, or the probability of success for any situation. Pendulums can be used to **make** accurate business decisions, best consumer choices, or career moves. They can assist in **determining** sex of unborn children, plant & soil deficiencies, and diagnostics for repairs of your house and automobiles. Finally, these tools can be instrumental in analyzing the physical, emotional, mental, and etheric body of either yourself or others including all needs, deficiencies, imbalances, patterns, fears, or blockages. In other words, these tools allow us to access the Infinite Intelligence or collective consciousness, opening the door to our own innate wisdom and to the consciousness of all humankind. This allows us the ability to have access to information or the answers to any questions that we can imagine. The pendulum and dowsing rods act as the means to make what we know in our intuition available to our conscious mind. The pendulum has been used by many people throughout history to externalize the intuition to determine an almost infinite amount of information and knowledge that is considered "the unknowns".

A "sample" or "witness" is a reference to the object of a specific test, or line of questioning. This "witness" can be just about anything: soil, copper, gold, vitamins, food, water, or colors. Whatever it may be, it is advisable to lay down a clean piece of paper on your table before placing the object on it to prevent residual vibrations being left on the table after the object is removed.

Testing Water: In testing water for purity, hold the pendulum over a cup of water. If it gyrates positively (clockwise) the water is pure and fit to drink. Counter-clockwise indicates that the water is in some way polluted and not fit to drink. Test: You can test a row of a dozen cups of water, one having salt (1 teaspoon) mixed in it, that is unknown to the tester. This is a good test for development of accuracy.

Food Testing: It is good to test your food before buying it in the store. You can determine whether the foods have been sprayed with chemicals, or exposed to radiation. You can determine the quality of the food, if it is organic or inorganic or whether you have an allergic reaction to that particular type of food. It all has to do with your specific line of questioning. The fluorescent lighting in a store could affect your test results, as could the other shoppers. It is probably best to do most of your in-depth testing at home.

It is easy to check for harmony or compatibility of your foods, vitamins, supplements, or anything else that you consume with the following technique.

Food Testing Technique

Adjust your pendulum over the food. When it is gyrating, hold your left hand, palm down, between the pendulum and the food. For most people, the normal response of the pendulum to the back of the hand should be a clockwise or positive gyration. If the pendulum continues to gyrate in a clockwise direction after you put your left hand over the food in question, thus indicates that there is harmony between you and the food. Should the gyrations change direction from positive to negative, or (clockwise to counter-clockwise), then that food is definitely *not* good for you, or not good for you at that time. If it changes to a side to side oscillation, this also indicates that it is not necessarily good or compatible for you.

Here is a case we have found to be quite common: A woman with unexplainable headaches went to a doctor, who could not find any reason for them. The woman tried a pendulum over her food and found clockwise for brown bread, boiled eggs, etc...and counter-clockwise for white bread, fried eggs, sugar, etc. She promptly changed her diet and to this day no longer has headaches.

It is very important to check your household products, your cosmetics and soaps, your cleansers, and anything with deodorants in it. Many of the products we use today contain harmful chemicals that can be the cause of allergies, rashes, headaches, or even low energy.

Testing products such as foods, vitamins, herbs, and remedies in relationship to yourself is done by holding the object or substance in your left hand and holding the pendulum over it. Again, the motions of the pendulum will be the same: clockwise is positive, compatible, harmonious, or good for you, and counter-clockwise is negative and not good, incompatible, or inharmonious for you. If *comparing two things* that are closely related, both being positive, you can gauge the difference by the

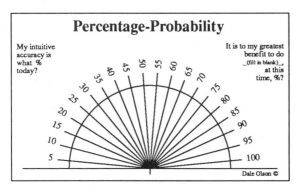

degree or number of the gyrations. The greater the degree of movement, or the greatest number of gyrations indicates a more positive or negative answer.

Another way to determine differences between many potential items of choice is to ask the intuition to assign a percentage of goodness that this particular product holds for you. This will allow you to test the differences between as many items as you would like and be able to choose between items of close likeness. For example, when testing of a shelf full of vitamins, minerals, or whatever, you may come up with such levels of goodness ratings as, 55%, 65%, 80%, 85%, 90%, and finally the winner being 98%. Use of the **Percentage Pendulum Chart** helps to make this process very quick and effective. When you are doing your testing, keep in mind that your *answer is for the immediate time only*. Your results may be different at another time with regard to a particular food, so check often until you have established a constance. This is especially important in regard to food allergies.

Figuring Quantity & Time Factor: While you are holding the substance in your left hand, ask: It is to my highest and greatest benefit to take, for example, Vitamin C, 100 mg., 500 mg., 1000 mg., etc. Then figure in the **Time factor:** It is best for me to take this once, twice, three, four...times a day, for one, two, three, four days....one week, two, three....one month, two, three... It is not necessarily good to take vitamins too often for you could be telling the body to shut down its natural production of a particular vitamin. Sometimes taking too much of a particular vitamin can be worse than not taking any at all. It is best to find out how often: "It is to my highest and greatest benefit to take this for, one, two, three weeks **ON**, and one, two weeks **OFF**, etc... " To check an unknown quantity and time variable you can do this with a pendulum. Hold the substance while checking these unknown variables, and count the positive gyrations. You can also use the backward and forward **Yes** answer with the pendulum when counting: 1, 2, 3, and 4. Perhaps when you get to 5, the swing will start going toward the **Maybe** direction, which is between the **Yes/No** direction. Then you back off to 4, and you see the swing return to **Yes**. It is good to recheck your answers often and to record the results.

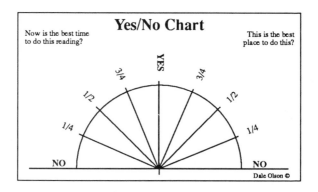

Yes/No Chart

Now is the best time to do this reading?

This is the best place to do this?

YES
3/4   3/4
1/2   1/2
1/4   1/4
NO   NO

Dale Olson ©

To have this ability to check all your foods, vitamins and supplements, or anything else that you take into your body, and to be able to take the guesswork out of it, is a very valuable skill. Prevention is better than the cure, so a little time and trouble spent on this may well be worthwhile as it will prove very beneficial to you in time, money, and quality of health. For further work with vitamins, minerals, quantity, and time factors, see the Pendulum Charts[3].

Direct Analysis from the Human Body: By holding the pendulum over the body you can detect any energy distortions which may be indicating an imbalance. Begin with a neutral swing (back and forth). The pendulum will respond to energy distortions or imbalances by either going to a **No** swing or to a counter-clockwise gyration. The energy normally flows up and down throughout the body and follows any curve, such as a bent arm. You can detect the negative conditions in the body involving any organ or gland by inquiring about functions and systems while moving the pendulum over the part and asking appropriate questions. The pain may give a negative energy distortion in one area, but the source may be somewhere else. For example, a headache may be caused by a digestion problem. See Pendulum Charts* for extensive testings of the human body.

Fertility Cycle: Some women use the pendulum to establish times of highest and lowest fertility for either conception or birth control. This is all right as long as you are not influencing the answers by an unconscious desire for a child or sex. If you are going to try this we would suggest you take a calendar and record your cycle objectively in advance. On the days that you have marked down as the ovulation time, pay close attention to any twinges or other sensations you may feel during ovulation. Keep a record of how accurate you are with your fertility cycle forecasting. This method has been accurate (greater than 80%) for those who have tried it. Again, it is suggested that this method be used only if you have had several months of accurate records to be sure you are not biasing your results due to unconscious desires. Having someone else besides the person in question do this method can increase the objectivity, resulting in an increase in the accuracy.

Sex Determination: The sex of an unborn child or animal can easily be determined by using the **Yes** swing (or clockwise) for a male, the **No** swing (or counterclockwise) for female. In the case of multiple births, it is also possible in the line of questioning to determine how many males, and how many females are in an animal's litter. First, establish how many there are in all by asking if there are 1,2,3, and so forth. Then determine the number of males and females. Even the time of birth can accurately be determined.

Animal Test: You can test animals as well, using the pendulum over the pets. This has been done at an egg ranch in Southern California. The pendulum is used over the eggs to determine whether the egg is fertile or not, or whether it contains a male or female chick. The egg production at this ranch has increased immensely. They found that the pendulum user at this ranch can do this type of testing for six hours or more with total accuracy. Point the egg to the North, keeping your hand on the table near the egg. A longitudinal swing means sterile, clockwise gyration means a male, counterclockwise means a female chick. This principle can be applied to a myriad of testing procedures for animals including feeds, medications, and diagnosing health problems.

Agricultural: Use of the pendulum and this technique will give you a better return on your labor by planting the right thing in the right place, and by using the right fertilizer or soil additives. The objective is to determine whether harmony exists between the plant and the soil, and between the plant and the fertilizer. If a plant is not in harmony with the soil in which it has been planted, it will grow but it will not thrive. That is common knowledge to all of us, but usually we have to find out for ourselves by trial and error. With the intuition, we can find the answer in a few minutes.

To Test Soil: On a piece of paper, place a small sample of the soil from the plot of ground that you are gardening, (a large handful is sufficient). About 18" away from the pile of soil, place your plant or seedling. Hold the pendulum over the soil and watch for a strong gyration of the pendulum. Then move the pendulum over the plant and watch the gyrations closely. If the gyrations are clockwise and increase when the pendulum is placed over the plant, then the soil is in harmony with the plant, and is therefore suitable for growing. If the gyrations are clockwise and decrease, it means that the soil is not particularly good, although not necessarily bad for the purpose. Should the pendulum change over to oscillations of forwards and backwards it signifies that the soil requires some form of fertilizer to make it suitable. If, however, the pendulum gyrates the opposite direction when held over the plant, then the soil is unsuitable and no attempt should be made to use it. This test can be applied to anything that grows in the ground, but a living specimen must be used as a sample. If there is an indication that some sort of fertilizer is needed to compensate for some deficiencies, then try the following test.

Test 2 Nutrient Balance: Have samples of about two ounces of each of the fertilizers or soil additives you may use. Place each substance several inches apart so as to be clear of each other's influence. Hold the pendulum over the plant. When it is gyrating clockwise, move it above each fertilizer and see which one gives the strongest reaction by the stronger gyrations or the number of gyrations. Now determine how much is required to be added to the heap of soil. Slowly add fertilizer in small measured amounts to the heap of soil, and the gyrations will increase. When the maximum is reached the gyrations will decrease. Careful measurement will give exact proportions of fertilizer to soil, for too much can also be detrimental. This method can be used for any nutrients you may wish to use to supplement your plant or animal kingdom.

Automobiles: Hold your pendulum over the engine, with the engine not running. While the pendulum is gyrating in a clockwise direction, begin to touch the various parts of the engine with your left hand, such as battery, valves, plugs, carburetor, etc. When a faulty part is touched, the pendulum will come to a stop, or go to a **No** oscillation of side-to-side, or go into a counter-clockwise gyration. This procedure has been very successful in diagnosing engine or car problems.

There are some dowsers who tune cars with the pendulum as finely as the best in diagnostic and tune-up equipment. One such dowser by the name of Marcel Trieau has illustrated this talent many times at the American Society of Dowsers convention. He simply points his finger to various parts of the engine and asks his Intuition to indicate whether that part is in order or not. He can also tell if that particular part is in only so-so shape by the rotation intensity of the pendulum. The fact that Trieau is a skilled mechanic makes a good combination of a skilled intellect and the intuition to make the proper complex calculations through past knowledge and experiences. In other words, he was asking the correct questions from the intellect in order to acquire the correct results from the intuition.

Generally speaking, answers are greatly aided by the skill, experience, and stored knowledge of the subconscious mind on the subject being tested. This previous procedure can also be used on your house or any other mechanical or electrical equipment.

Harmful radiations: You will find it interesting to test your TV set or microwave oven to see how far it gives off harmful radiations. With your pendulum start as far back as possible, slowly walk towards the object you are testing and watch where the movement of the pendulum changes to negative, then check from the side. With the television on, I have found the noxious radiations to be as far reaching as 6 to 10 feet, and with microwave oven, 4 to 8 feet. It is advisable not to let children, animals or yourself, sit within that noxious energy field. Over time, these harmful radiations can be a factor in causing health disorders. They can also have an adverse effect by weakening the immune system.

High power electrical lines are also stressful on the human body. Adverse health problems are often a result of living too close to high power electrical lines. High power electrical lines are believed to create direct interference with the central nervous system and can cause neuromuscular confusion, disorientation, and abnormal distribution and absorption of minerals. In our testing with overhead AC electrical power lines, we have found that adverse effects on the human body can be felt as close as 35-40 feet for 2,000 volt lines, and 340-350 feet for 230,000 volt lines. You may want to check out the range of adverse effects of overhead power lines before buying a house. With the use of a pendulum and dowsing rods you can now check out these unseen fields of harmful noxious radiations from your T.V., computers, heaters, ceiling heat, e.t.c..

Direction Finding: When you are outdoors, your pendulum can be used to tell you where North is. Simply hold your left arm up, and if you have a set of keys, hold them in your left hand between your first and third finger, dangling downwards (these will act as an aerial), and point with your left index finger. Hold your pendulum in your right hand, and slowly turn around in a circle. The pendulum will oscillate until you notice a large swing indicating north and a shorter swing pointing to the south. The pendulum indicates direction because you are working with the electromagnetic energy of the earth, which runs North and South. Do check this technique out with a compass for accuracy before you get lost.

Business Decisions: On the job and in business, using the intuition can give you a great advantage over the normal trial and error approach to decision making. If you are wavering between two alternatives in a business decision, you can use your intuition, pendulum, and **Yes/ No,** or **Percentage Charts** to find the best course of action. Using the Intuition is an excellent way to help give you a boost in making up your mind. Additional applications would be to use the intuition in locating a specific area or item such as a building site for a business, the perfect store front, the right tool or truck.

Another use of the intuition in business would be for finding the perfect employee for a particular job. Finding the best employee to hire can be very tedious, time consuming, and the best employee may not always be apparent from the application. This task can be greatly facilitated by taking your pile of applications and resumes, reading the name of the applicant, and scanning the pages of the application. Put your left (receiving) hand over the signature or photo, use your pendulum and **Percentage Chart**, determine to what degree this applicant will be best suited to fill the open position, assign a percentage to this individual and move on to the next applicant. We have found this to be very effective and accurate, especially when there are many closely qualified candidates and the determining factor cannot be gauged from the application.

The intuition can also be used in sales to locate prospects and prospective areas, or in land deals where it may be necessary to determine water or minerals. One of the most effective uses of the pendulum has been in telephone conversations where a snap decision needs to be made, or in understanding what the person on the other end of the line is trying to say, or in determining the validity or truth of what is being said.

The ability to use your intuition to weigh the pros and cons of any situation before making a business decision can save you a great deal of time, effort, and money. The more you use and develop your intuition, the more you will find ways to use it in business or personal life applications, thereby creating greater quality and success in your life.

Years ago, I had a construction company and needed to make contracting bids on a regular basis. For many in the business, this was a procedure that could take one day to one or more weeks of detailed planning, telephone time and footwork to determine the end or total figure to submit to the customer. In most cases, if the contractor didn't get the job, all the time required to make the bid was uncompensated. After having been in the trades for quite a few years, I did have a fairly good idea as to the cost of things; nonetheless, I didn't like all the time it took for figuring bids and estimates. I started to use my intuition and pendulum to determine the right cost figure of the job for both myself and the customer. After checking out the job site and talking with the potential customer, I would go out to my van and come up with the right figure. At first, to determine the right figure, I would ask: "How badly do I need this job?", "How tough is the competition?", "Can the customer afford what their ideas will cost?" However, I found that this type of questioning could be somewhat fear laden, and that could possibly have had a negative effect on the results of the test.

A more inclusive type of questioning that I found to give the best results was; "It would be to my highest and greatest benefit to take on this job with _____ (customer name)", if **Yes**, then, "Infinite, indicate the perfect cost figure of this job for _____ (customer) that will be for the highest and greatest benefit of _____ (customer) and myself" This procedure would take me a whole five minutes, and to my customer's surprise I would come back with the bid or estimate in hand. The interesting thing about all of this was, first of all, I had nothing but really great customers. Secondly, I always got the job. The surprised looks on the faces of my customers were always fun, for they looked like I had just read their mind down to the cents, with comments like; "Well, that's exactly what I had in mind, when can you start?"

Sometimes the jobs ended up taking more time or more money, but, usually the customers were great about it and balanced out the overrun cost. As the result of using and trusting in my intuition, I know beyond any question of doubt that I made better decisions in a fraction of the time, and I saved my customers and myself a great deal of time and money with a minimum amount of stress. The intuition was also incredibly helpful in on-the-job trouble shooting, usually leaving the customers and the other tradespeople dumbfounded as to how I was able to solve the problem so quickly even with so many unknown factors.

With practice and common sense, you will learn what the pendulum (intuition) will and will not answer for you. Much will depend on where your limitations are in your thinking or belief systems at any particular time or place.

If you would like instruction to further your development in using the pendulum (including applications for any choice, decision or determination regarding yourself, others, animals, plants or objects) see Advanced Pendulum Instruction and Applications, and Knowing Your Intuitive Mind: Pendulum Charts and Applications available from: D.W. Olson Crystalline Publications P.O. Box 2088 Eugene, Or. 97402

---

[3] **Knowing Your Intuitive Mind, Pendulum Charts**, D.W. Olson, Crystalline Publications, Eugene, OR.

Chapter 9
USING DOWSING RODS

Dowsing usually refers to the search for water or minerals by using one or more rods or a stick to externalize the intuition. However, in this case, we will be using the art of dowsing much more extensively. Dowsing is a mind-expanding experience. In dowsing, one must be able to reach out with the mind to include the vibration, frequency or the essence of that which is being tested. The Micro Breath is helpful for assisting you in keeping the ego or intellect out of the picture. It is important to not let your intellect hypothesize the results of a test. For example, " I believe that the object of the test is over here or over there." It is a matter of learning how to push out any unwanted thoughts and stay completely focused on the objective. Learning to concentrate completely in this way will work in developing your skill in dowsing.

Learning to use L-rods is like learning any other skill of the intuition. It requires time, determination, trust, balance, and persistent practice. Given these, your success is guaranteed. The parameters are the same as with all other tools of the intuition. Every object, animate or inanimate, gives off energetic radiations which our expanded senses can feel, and we can measure with the following techniques. The subconscious, intuitive or super-conscious mind is the recipient, of the information, which is then translated into nerve impulses to the muscle tissue, with the result being a slight movement of the dowsing rods.

The L-rods (dowsing rods) are a communication device between the conscious and the subconscious mind. Therefore, it is a matter of establishing the language between these two parts of the mind. It takes time and practice for the subconscious to understand what is expected of it and respond accordingly. It is necessary to approach the L-rods with enthusiasm, optimism, and the confidence that you are able to effectively use them as intuitive measuring devices. Unlike the pendulum, which relies on subtle muscular movements initiated by the intuition, the language of the L-rods has more to do with balance. For some, the use of L-rods comes very easily and with others it takes a lot of practice to establish the balance and the communication codes between the conscious and subconscious.

We have seen many different shapes and sizes of dowsing rods. The simplest design is a straight L-shaped rod with a 3-to-1 ratio dimension. In emergency situations, we have even used coat hangers cut to the proper length ratio. After many prototypes, we feel very comfortable with a brass rod with handles that allow for maximum sensitivity and freedom for easy movement. As with pendulums, there are many types of rods and dowsing apparatus available, however, it is not the instrument that is doing the finding, it is your intuition. It comes down to whether it is a (Y) rod, a set of L-rods, or "whatchamacallits", and it is really a matter of which one you feel the most comfortable with and trust.

We have found that the L-rods can be most effective in measurement of the energetic fields and chakras of the human body. This we will expand on in greater detail later in this chapter. We suggest you first develop your intuitive dowsing abilities with the simple L- rods, and then if you feel so inclined, try a variety of other dowsing tools. Again, the object of the instrument is to indicate to you what you already know a split second earlier via the nerve impulses and muscle movement from your own intuition and physical body.

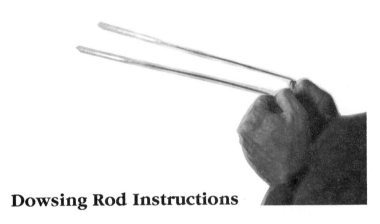

Dowsing Rod Instructions

Beginning Dowsing

1. The breath is a very effective tool in balancing the mental, emotional and physical bodies (see Micro Breath). For balance, breathe in deeply, and release any negative or critical thoughts about the outcome of your test by breathing them out through your mouth slowly. Breath in through your nose, release out through your mouth slowly until you feel emotionally and mentally balanced.

2. It takes time to get use to holding and balancing the rods so that they don't swing wildly. Hold the rods firmly, but not tightly, with your hands comfortably around the handles with your index fingers down at least 1/2 inch from the top of

the handles. With one rod in each hand, find a comfortable position. For most, this will be somewhere in the area from the bottom of the breast bone to the navel. Keep the rods parallel to the ground plane, with the tips of the rods one half to one inch below the level point. This will help to keep the rods from swinging out of control. If your rods are pointed too high in relationship to the parallel point, the rods will swing open. If your rods are pointed to low, the rods will have an extra resistance to overcome and it will be hard for them to open in response to the energy testing. To give you a little extra support and balance, bring your gripped hands together so that they are lightly touching and supporting each other. Your elbows tucked against your waist will also give you greater stability.

Rods crossing indicating closed off energy field or chakra.

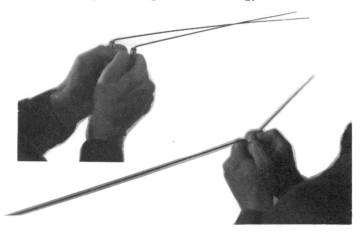

Rods completely open indicating boundry line of energy field or chakra completely open.

3. To find the point of balance, start with your rods pointing slightly downward and bring them upward slowly to the point where the rods begin to open up or swing apart. Now, ever so slightly bring them back down slowly to the point of balance. Again, the Micro Breath helps to maintain balance on all levels. Once you learn this point of balance from practice, you will be able to find this reference point easily. It also helps to lock your rods by putting your thumbs on the top of the L-rods to prevent them from swinging until you bring them up to the balance point. Then release your thumbs. This helps to stabilize the rods before putting them into action. L-rods without handles should be held as loosely as possible while still maintaining the control and balance necessary for the outward swing of the L-rods.

4. The next step is to learn how to walk with them, softly, evenly, without jarring your rods out of balance.

5. In order to prevent lack of response, it helps to defocus your attention from the rods. Remain neutral or objective to the results, and continue to do the Micro Breath to offset any possible auto-suggestion from the mental or logical mind. Focus your intention with your mind on that which you wish to test or find and establish the language between your conscious and unconscious mind. It helps to speak the intentions out loud to your subconscious mind. In order to obtain the most accurate results. It is imperative that you *be precise, specific, positive, and affirmative when you communicate with your subconscious.* For example:"Intuitive mind, indicate the direction of North." This can be indicated by one or both

of your rods swinging to the North direction. Then check with a compass for accuracy. Repeat this exercise (or do another test for an unknown variable that you can verify with another means of measurement) a few times each day throughout the following seven days and note your consistency in results. In finding water or electrical lines, it is not necessary to point downward or at the object. It is best to keep your rods balanced or parallel to the ground plane. Remember, it is your intuitive mind that is doing the measuring, and not the rods. They are simply the indicators. In the beginning it is best to practice for short periods of 20 minutes or less.

6. If you have difficulty in making the rods move or in being consistent, then consider that you may be unwittingly affecting the test. If you are tired, forcing the situation, or in an imbalanced state, you may accidently affect the results. If so, give it a rest and approach it at another time.

7. Any thoughts about the possible answer, personal desires, feelings about the outcome, ego involvement, or tendency to show off will influence the accuracy of your work. Keeping yourself objective and detached from the outcome is one of the keys to your success.

8. When you have completed your dowsing session, it is always helpful to give thanks to your intuition and Infinite Intelligence for being of service.

A good dowser does not just see the answers in the movement of the rods. They also feel or sense the answers in terms of frequency registrations in their hands, arms, or entire body. As you practice with doing some mock finds, pay close attention to the inner sensation of "pulling" that occurs just before the rods begin to swing open. Keep this sensation as a reference point within your conscious awareness. It is a response of the centers within your body indicating your inner ability to sense the results of answers to the test before the actual response of the dowsing tools. Encourage the development of this inner subtle sensing. This inner subtle sensing will be a great asset to you as you become more proficient in doing accurate finds.

You can practice the technique of finding by having someone bury a personal object like a ring or something metallic, and practice locating it. Start simply and build this ability slowly. Setting yourself too great a challenge at the start can be discouraging if it doesn't work out. Start out by setting the parameters of the "find zone" or "find point" in a small area, such as a section of your front yard.

The Subdivision Dowsing Technique

Choose one edge or boundary of the test area, preferably at the center point of that boundary line, and draw some imaginary lines out from your standing point subdividing the entire test area into sections like that of a sunburst pattern.

1. Balance your L-rods in hands.

2. Bring yourself to center or balance with the Pulsed Breath.

3. While maintaining the Micro Breath, focus your attention on that which you are attempting to find. Hold the visualization completely in your mind.

4. Hold your rods balanced, parallel to the ground and parallel to each other, slightly open.

5. While keeping your attention focused, turn yourself and the rods with easy, gentle movements so as to not jar your rods in the direction of your attention and check each section of the subdivided test area.

6. When you get to the segment with the object you are searching for, the rods will begin to open up slowly, or cross depending on your line of communication. You can continue to check other segments, but, you will definitely get a stronger reaction in the one segment were the test object lies. Of course, if the object you are searching for lies in more than one segment, you may get an equal reaction in two or more segments.

7. Begin to walk the length of the segment where you received the strongest response. Continue to walk slowly until you find the rods either opening up completely, or closing down and crossing. This depends on what communications you have established with your subconscious as a Yes/No answer (either X marks the spot with the rods crossing, or the rods open completely at the right location). When you get a strong response with your L-rods, move forwards, backwards, or side to side to test for a stronger or weaker response. You now will most likely be at the find spot. This technique can be applied to most forms of lost or buried objects.

8. Locating misplaced personal articles around the house can especially be good practice in developing this skill. Simply create the intention to find the article in your mind, hold your balanced rods and slowly turn around until you get a response with your rods in one particular direction. Keep your mind concentrated on the object until you become aware of the "correct direction". The direction will simply feel right. The distance you are from the object you are searching for has nothing to do with your success.

L-Rods: Applications

Finding Buried Power, Water, or Gas Lines:

Finding water pipes, underground electrical cables or gas pipes can be one of the best ways to build confidence with dowsing, because they are usually easier to find than most objects and because you can get immediate feedback by verifying the location with another source of information. Practice this technique as you build your confidence in dowsing.

To find buried pipes or cables, instruct your subconscious mind or intuition through your conscious verbal affirmations to direct the rods to turn outwards when your feet or the handles cross over the particular pipe or line of the test. For example, "Infinite, indicate through me and the rods the exact location of the buried _____ pipe." Keeping your rods balanced, stare down past the rods intently. Your focus point is not the rods, but beyond them with an almost defocusing of what is directly in front of you. The focus is on your questioning or visualization of the object. Now walk slowly in the direction of where you feel the buried pipe is located. Maintain your focused attention or concentration on the pipe. If it is a water pipe, then concentrate not on just any water pipe, but specifically on the water in the water pipe for which you are searching. As your feet cross over the pipe, the rods will swing out at right angles or will cross, depending on what directions you have established with your subconscious mind. If the rods are sluggish, or if one responds strongly and the other to a lesser degree, this will correct itself with time and practice. Such discrepancies usually indicate the need for greater integration of your directions to the subconscious mind, which will lead to a greater coordination of the subtle muscle movements responsible for influencing the L-rods.

Another good practice would be to do some testing for buried pipes within a city neighborhood where there are both underground water and gas pipes going to each house. Simply walk down the sidewalk with your rods and selectively test for water or gas independently. When the rods respond, look to see where the meter is for the water or gas to that house. You will find it interesting that we have the ability to selectively choose whether we are dowsing for water, gas, or whatever. For example, you may get a find response to the water test you are conducting and get no response to the gas pipe that may be 6 inches away. This selective programming to the subconscious mind depends on both your ability to give precise, specific directions of intent and also your concentration on the objective of the test. The discovery of your ability to detect or find objects or substances just by selectively using your intuitive mind will be one of your greatest thrills.

Finding Water: Dowsing for water can be easy since water gives such strong response. Information on water dowsing is available from skilled dowsers. However, there is a vast amount of knowledge you would need to have about water and water tables before you start drilling a potential well site. Water occurs in many formations. There are various types of soil, porous, sand, gravel where water sinks into the ground. For example, water may lie in an aquifer made up of sand and/or gravel with a ceiling of clay. Depending on the part of the country, the depth of the well may range anywhere from a few feet to thousands of feet to find potable water. Determine if the water is potable, or whether it is contaminated by salt, bacteria, heavy metal, or harmful chemicals. There are good or potable water "domes", water "ovals", and water veins that can handle your water needs. There are also very shallow accumulated underground water reservoirs that will not stand up to the required demand. It is obvious that you must learn as much as possible about water and ground formations before you take up serious water dowsing.

As with all other aspects of communications with the intuition, the accuracy of your answers will depend on the preciseness and specifics of your questions, and your clear focus or concentration on the line of questioning. Don't let this discourage you from just going out and checking your property for water, for who's going to be more unconsciously attuned to your own property than yourself. There is always beginner's luck.

There is an interesting article in the November, 1970 *Mother Earth News*. Mrs J.P. Pendergrass of Raleigh, N.C. does her "water witching" in suburban Laurel Hills. She found her own well and says, "It's the best one in the development. I witched two others out here, and one of them is real good. The well driller wouldn't go where I told him to on the other one, though, and they haven't got enough water."

Locating water can be as simple as using the Subdivision Technique described earlier and simply searching while walking the land keeping in mind a clear picture of pure water with a sufficient supply (6 gallons per minute or more) at a reasonable depth. At the "find point" you can then determine whether you have found an underground stream, water dome, or underground spring. You can also determine the available water and depth. A pendulum can be a helpful tool in determining specifics at close range.

Finding Gold: As I mentioned in the note from the author, it is possible to find gold by dowsing. But, dowsing for gold can be very tricky, largely due to the vested interest in a successful outcome. Remember, it is imperative to detach from the ego so that the intuition can shine through unimpeded. Gold fever can be one of the hardest emotions to overcome, yet it is not impossible.

It would be helpful to learn about mineralogy, geology, and prospecting as you start your search.

Have a sample of placer gold or "witness", and allow the frequency or vibration of gold be a known variable in your unconscious mind. This understanding of the subtle gold vibration comes with subtle sensing practice and exposure to gold buried beneath the ground. You could practice by having someone bury a sample piece of adequate size and using the Subdivision Technique to find it. After you develop the skill, you could walk old stream beds or river banks in areas where there is a history of gold finds. Fine metal detectors are on the market and sometimes they are available for rental. It is recommended to use both techniques, especially when it involves digging holes that may be greater than two feet deep. Before getting too carried away, a second opinion is suggested before bringing in the heavy equipment and tearing up the landscape.

Detecting Harmful Radiations: Dowsing rods work very well for detecting harmful radiations from microwave, television, power lines, and ley lines. With your rods, start as far back as possible from the object you are testing and slowly walk towards the object. Watch the point where the rods begin to open. Back up from this point, and the rods will most likely close back to the parallel or starting point. Where the rods begin to open is the beginning of the unseen field of harmful or noxious energy.

There has been limited research on the adverse effects of microwave and other high power radiations; however, the intuition and some of our case research has provided us with enough valid information to lead us to believe it is important to bring to your awareness the possible adverse effects of these radiations present in our everyday life. With a microwave oven we have seen the field extend as far as 4 to 8 feet. This can also be verified with a compass, since microwave ovens work on a high level of electromagnetism. Some of the physically tangible effects of microwave ovens can occur when children or adults stand directly in front of the microwave oven and watch the food cook. The very minute amount of microwave that leaks out is known to have a clouding effect upon the cornea of the eye, creating premature cataracts of the eyes.

In the measurement of television or computer monitors, we have found the positive ion of radiation to extend as far out as 4 to 8 feet. Positive charged ions have a weakening effect on the body's stress-fighting immune system by neutralizing the negative ions from the body's Bio-Energy reserve. Increased positive ions increase one's irritability, nervousness, or anxiety. Find out for yourself how far the positive ions radiate out from your television, and create your own arbitrary safety margin area where you, your children and your pets don't sit.

The radiation from overhead high power lines is more noticeable even to the conscious mind. Have you ever stood under some high power lines for any length of time? How did you feel, especially the top of your head or the pit of your stomach? Did you notice how maybe your teeth were clenched together? What do you think your body was telling you? Perhaps your body felt the need to get away or protect itself by covering the top of your head with your hand or something. At the very extreme, there was a case where the three children of a family were constantly sick with various illness and missing many days of school. The high power lines were observed to be within 40 feet of the house, and the parents were advised to relocate to another house. What was interesting about this case is that once these children were relocated away from the power lines, they regained total health and didn't miss any more days for the rest of the school year.

Our bodies work on an electromagnetic energy system, and anytime we spend too much time near such high energy sources, we subject ourselves to possible disruption of our own energy harmonics. These adverse effects can create direct interference with the central nervous system and cause neuromuscular confusion, disorientation, abnormal distribution and absorption of minerals, and a reduction in your immune system resulting in a possible increase of disorder or disease. In testing with overhead AC electrical power lines, it has been found that negative reactions in the human body occur at the following distances: 35-40 feet for 2,000 volt lines, 340-350 feet for 230,000 volt lines, etc. You may want to check out the adverse effect range of overhead power lines before buying a house. With the use of dowsing rods you can now check out these unseen fields of harmful radiation. In checking out all radiation, the technique is to start far enough away, keep yourself centered and balanced by continuing to do the Micro Breath as you walk slowly, keep your rods parallel to the ground, and watch for your L-rods to open.

Auric Fields Reading: By using L-rods, we have the ability to measure the auric or the energetic field that surrounds the body of humans, animals, or plants. This field not only surrounds our bodies, but extends out from them depending on general health, energy level, and vitality. This energy field can be measured by some technologically advanced equipment, captured on film with Kirilian photography, or seen by some individuals with expanded sight. For most people, the auric field extends out anywhere from 2 to 10 feet or more. This is not an indicator of the quality of the field, it merely shows how far the field extends. The field can shut down if exposed to harmful radiation or negative energy. Measuring the auric field can be an extremely accurate and instant gauge on the effects of certain substances (food, vitamins, medication, etc.) in relationship to the well-being of the body. This type of measurement can also be very useful in determining the effectiveness of a particular therapy or remedy. To determine the effectiveness in any of these cases, simply measure the auric field both before and after the introduction of the substance, therapy, or remedy.

The key to successful and accurate readings of the auric field is the same as is required when using other means to externalize the intuition:

1. Focus on the objective, keep the intention clear. Maintain balance by exercising the Micro Breath. To do this type of testing, stand back about 10 feet or more and face the individual you are going to test.

2. At the start, use the Pulse Breath to clear and balance your own mind and emotions. Now you are ready to proceed with your testing.

3. First, measure the baseline of the individual in question. Do this by having the individual hold their right hand over their breast bone (heart chakra, thymus gland) and stand relaxed. Now,

you as the Tester draw in your breath with the intention to measure how far this individual's auric field extends from their body and begin doing the Micro Breath.

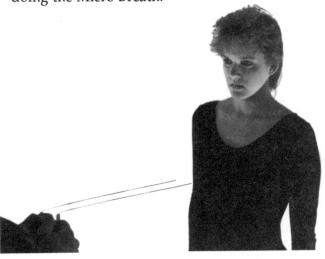

4. Slowly bring your L-rods up to parallel or point of balance, and walk carefully to prevent jarring your rods. Walk towards the person that you are testing, keeping your focus on your objective and seeing beyond the rods. When you get to the beginning of their auric field the rods will begin to open.

5. Now, draw an imaginary line on the floor at the point where the rods are completely open. This will indicate how far the auric field extends from that individual's body and will indicate their general health and vitality. This is the reference point or baseline for comparative analysis.

6. The next step would be to repeat the test, except this time your questioning is based on the increase in general health or vitality to the individual as a result of the therapy or remedy. The comparison is of the auric field before (baseline) and after the therapy or remedy. You can use this technique in a myriad of ways to test for just about anything that you can think of.

Food & Substance Test: You can use the L-rods for checking whether a substance such as a food, vitamin, medication, or crystal is for your highest and greatest benefit. Simply place the substance over the Thymus/ Heart center. This is called the "Witness" area. You can then test how much the field opens or closes in comparison to your first baseline test. The technique is the same as in the above testing, except in the second comparative test, the substance is held by the individual being tested in their right hand over the "Witness" area (breast bone, heart chakra). Do the test again and compare the increase or decrease in the auric field with the substance in question. This can be extremely useful in checking out the "goodness" of all products that you consume, or substances for your body or environment.

First test: without the substance to establish the baseline (natural distance of auric field).

Second test: have the individual hold the substance in their right hand over their Witness area. Notice the increase or decrease in the individual's auric field as a result of the substance in question.

Chakra Reading: The chakra system has been seen to be an extremely accurate gauge of the wellness of an individual. The chakras are electrical magnetic energetics that are precise indicators of an individual's total health. You can not hide anything in this type of testing. All weaknesses, patterns, imprints, traumas, disorders, or diseases can be gauged or seen through the chakra system of the body. L-rods can be an accurate tool in measuring which of the 7 major chakras of the body are closed down or blocked. Consequently the L-rods can indicate the well being of the physical, mental, emotional, and spiritual parts of the individual. Each chakra has various emotional and mental aspects and attributes associated with it. These energy vortices can be measured with the L-rods and can accurately indicate what is going on in that region of the body. The L-rods indicate what physical, emotional, or mental issues, vicious circles, patterns, unresolved conflicts, or blocked energy are associated with that particular chakra.

The information on the Chakra systems is extensive and would take volumes to explore; nonetheless, we do want to give you the basic information about the chakra system to get you started. The following are basic aspects and attributes associated with each chakra:

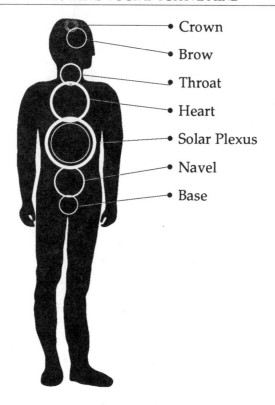

Crown

Brow

Throat

Heart

Solar Plexus

Navel

Base

1. **Base Center**: located at the base of spine. Function: survival, grounding, instincts.

2. **Navel-Spleen Center**: Located at the lower abdomen, genitals, womb. Function: desire, pleasure, sexuality, nurturance, lower emotions (self-worth, self-esteem, confidence, deservabilty, worthiness).

3. **Solar Plexus Center**: Located at the navel to solar plexus. Function: personal power, will, action, emotions, and gut feelings.

4. **Heart Center**: Located at the heart. Function: love, compassion, balance. Governor between upper and lower parts of the body and realities.

5. **Throat Center**: Located at the throat. Function: communications, creativity, self-expression.

6. **Brow, Ajna, Third Eye Center**: Located at the center of head slightly above eye level. Function: seeing, intuition, imagination.

7. **Crown Center**: Located at the top of head. Function: understanding, knowing, bliss.

The technique for measuring the chakras is similar to the method for measuring the Auric Field. Face the individual from about 10 to 12 feet away. Use the Pulse Breath to clear and center yourself before each test for each and every chakra. After you do the Pulse Breath for centering, draw in your breath to do the Micro Breath and with that breath, draw in your intention to measure one of the 7 chakras. Always start with the Base chakra measurement and move to the 2nd, 3rd, 4th, 5th, 6th, and 7th chakras. You do not need to point your L-rods in the direction of the chakras, simply direct your focus and intention to the particular chakra which you are testing. Keep your rods balanced. Proceed slowly toward the individual until the rods open up or close down and cross. These motions will measure how open or closed that particular chakra is. The closed or crossed rods indicate a congested or blocked chakra.

It is helpful to visualize the individual being tested as healthy and whole, thereby offsetting possible bias or projection from your own mind. This form of testing is extremely helpful in using before and after a particular type of therapy to determine it's effectiveness on the individuals total health. This form of testing is also helpful as an instant energetic feedback and allows one to begin focusing energy to the closed off areas to start one's own healing process. All disorder and all healing to the body can be seen first in the energetics of the auric field and the chakras of the body

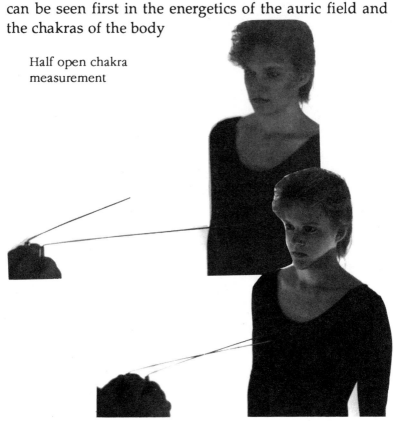

Half open chakra measurement

Closed chakra measurement indicating emotional or mental congestion, trauma, or issues associated with that chakra.

The rods indicate how open or closed the individual chakras are, and also show the energy differences between one side of the body and the other. Sometimes one side of the body is more open or closed (blocked) than the other side. This type of testing will show differences between one's masculine side (the right side of the body) and one's feminine side (the left side of the body), regardless of one's sex. One side being more open or closed can indicate one's unresolved issues with their masculine or feminine self, or it can indicate issues going back to unresolved conflicts with their mother or father. The information that you can obtain from measuring the chakras and auric field could fill volumes, and I encourage you to practice these techniques and let the tools and your intuition teach you what is true for you.

Chakras & Mirrors: It is possible to measure your own chakras by using a mirror on a wall. Mirrors are very reflective of energy, since they are made up of silver and silica. One can use a mirror to measure their own chakras with the above technique, thereby enabling yourself to measure your own progress with your process in life. For an extensive and accurate view on the chakra system, we would suggest reading "Wheels of Life" by Anodea Judith.

Chapter 10
MUSCLE TESTING: APPLIED BIOKINESIOLOGY

Muscle testing (Applied Biokinesiology) can help you take the guesswork out of choosing the proper foods, vitamins, herbs, medications, remedies, or objects that may or may not be for your greatest benefit. It enables you to test an individual's brain and body response for innate intuitive answers.

The muscle testing procedure was developed by Doctor George Goodhart in the 1960's. He started by correlating muscle strengths or weaknesses to states of health. Extensive work with certain muscles indicated that if muscles were weak, or strong muscles became weak when certain acupuncture points were touched, then this would indicate what imbalances existed in the body. From there, Goodhart would determine what differences foods or food supplements would have on strengthening weak muscles and restoring balance to the body. Today, muscle testing as a procedure for analysis is wide-spread and is being used by professionals and laypeople alike to take the guesswork out of their approach to the human body.

The body's brain, and its interconnected circuits with the organs, muscles, and various tissues, determine the internal integrity of the body by running a complete systems check every few seconds. These connections or circuits are very helpful because they give us direct access to the brain's bank of knowledge about the condition of the whole body. This allows us to understand the reaction of the whole body to the environment and to specific input. In other words, there is a part of our mind that is totally aware of every balance and imbalance within every aspect of the whole body. It is this information that is completely available to the conscious mind by means of the intuition through the subconscious mind. This information is then transferred down to the response of certain muscles. It is through this response of the muscles that information can be communicated. In essence, muscle testing is nothing more than another means to communicate with an individual's intuition. In this method, the tester presses down on certain isolated muscles while asking a clear question about the individual being tested.

Illustration of proper wrist contact and hand/arm position of recipient.

In this procedure of muscle testing, the anterior deltoid (shoulder) muscle is being used as the indicator muscle. The food being tested can be placed either near the nerve terminals of the mouth (jaw point below ear lobe) or the navel while the strength of the muscle is tested again.

We are then able to determine what signal the nerve receptors are sending to the brain by the instant muscle reaction. If the indicator muscle weakens, the nerve centers are telling the brain that there is something wrong with the food. However, if the muscle maintains its energy level and does not weaken, then it is safe to say that the food in question is being accepted by the body as beneficial. On the other hand, if the energy level increases too much, indicating as being over-strong, we know that the nerve centers are cautioning the brain against possible damage due to excessive energy. This form of muscle testing can also be utilized with all sorts of nutritional questions, medicines, vitamins, minerals, herbs, homeopathics, crystals, gemstones or other objects. This same alarm system can also assist you in determining allergies to all that surrounds you, including the clothes you wear, and the materials of the building you live in. Also, it can detect pollution in the water you drink or the air you breathe.

Arm bouncing upward (over-strong) indicates weakness the same as arm dropping.

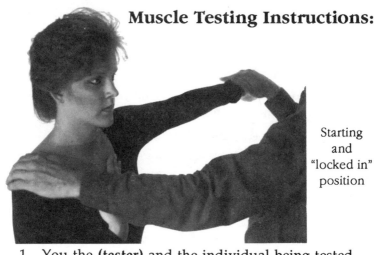

Muscle Testing Instructions:

Starting
and
"locked in"
position

1. You the **(tester)** and the individual being tested the **(recipient)** stand with your feet firmly placed about one foot apart **facing** each other's left or right shoulder   The preference of shoulder side is up to the tester as a matter of comfort or what side works best for that situation. Make sure that you do not stand right in front of each other. You can alternate between the right and left shoulder of the recipient so that you can prevent from over taxing the individuals arm throughout the testing.

2. You are standing about two feet away from each other, looking at your recipient's right shoulder (preference shoulder).

3. You place your right palm firmly on the recipient's left shoulder in order to stabilize it and begin a circuit for energy flow.

4. Have the recipient place their left hand (palm flat) over the **"witness"** area with their right arm at this point hanging loosely at their side. If the recipient is having the left arm used in the testing

then it would be the right hand over the witness area.

5. Have the recipient raise their left arm straight up to the side and slightly to the front—see diagram. It is very important that before you start, ask the recipient, "Is there anything wrong with this arm or shoulder (left arm in this test)?," "Have you had any physical injuries to this arm or shoulder?," and, "Is this arm okay for me to use for this test?" The other hand of the recipient should hang loosely, slightly flexed down from their extended arm. Their head and eyes should always look straight forward.

6. Now verbally communicate the intention of what it is that you are going to do with the individual that you are testing;

   a. "I would like you to hold your left hand (choice of side) palm flat, fingers extended over your breast bone."

   b. "I would now like you to stretch your right arm (choice of side) out with wrist bent, fingers extended with thumb pointing slightly down."

   c. "When I say **hold**, I would like you to prevent me from pushing your arm down. This is not a test of strength, so I would like you to not hurt your arm by straining."

   d. "We are going to first establish your baseline or strength point at normal condition."

   e. "Next, we will be testing this _____ (sample) to determine whether this is for your highest and greatest benefit."

7. To begin the test, first determine the "**baseline**". The baseline is to determine at what point the strength of arm of the recipient will "lock-in" place. You as the tester will press down with your left hand on the upper part of the individual's wrist (the wrist can be wetted for better conduction). You must put the palm of your hand on the back of the recipient's wrist joint (see diagram). Make sure that the recipient's opposite or free hand does not make a fist, curl the fingers, or point the fingers toward the body.

8. You need to learn to press very gently on the recipient's wrist while they resist. Just before pressing, say **"hold"** and then press down firmly, gently with the same amount of effort each time. It is a holding for only a second or two with only enough strength to move the arm down a half of an inch and let it bounce back to it's original position. You are **not** trying to overpower the other person. This is **not a test of strength** and you are not trying to pull muscles. It is not a contest but simply a friendly pressing movement that needs to only last a second or two to indicate to both of you the relative strength of the recipient's arm in a resistance position. Be gentle; test several times until both of you acquire a feel for the point of resistance where the arm feels strong and "locked-in". Press with the same effort each time. Memorize the amount of effort needed each time to find that "locked-in" point of resistance. You will notice after some practice that their arm will instantly respond to the "locked-in" position. With most people, you will have applied from 5 to 7 pounds of pressure. Practice with a scale by pressing down 5 to 7

pounds until you get that feel of applied pressure. Remember this is not a battle of strength.

9. Now that you have the "baseline," or locked-in position established, you can start checking different samples or the objective of your testing. Next you need to decide which "witness" area you are going to use. By "witness" area we mean that area which will give the greatest or most accurate response to that which is in question. In order to keep this simple and effective for you, we will use two "witness" areas for most of the testing, (see "witness area").

10. When the arm weakens in a test and begins to go down, while pressing 5 to 7 pounds of pressure, **always follow through with the pressure.** In other words, when the arm starts to go down— press it all the way down. It is a unique feeling

when the arm weakens that allows the individual being tested to know beyond any question of doubt that their body responded negatively to the substance or object in question by going completely weak.

Witness Area

There are several areas on the body that can serve as "witness areas." The "witness area" that you use will depend greatly on the type of information that you are accessing or the system of muscle testing that you utilize. Some *muscle testing systems* include using the touch of certain acupuncture points in conjunction with the muscle test, thereby indicating balance/imbalance of any part of

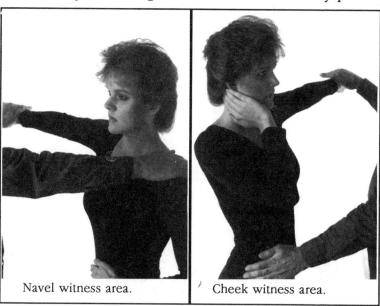

Navel witness area.　　　Cheek witness area.

the body (organs, muscles, tissue, system), or specific nutritional needs. This system is quite extensive and would require that you learn a great deal more than we will be addressing in this introductory level of muscle testing.

1. If your testing involves nutritional or food allergy questions, it would be suggested to use one of three places to place the food sample. The recipient of the test could either hold the food sample at the cheek (parotid), in their mouth, or at the navel. For this type of testing of foods for nutritional or allergic reactions, have the individual hold the nutrition on the parotid or navel area for at least 10 seconds before the actual test. If the method of placing samples in the mouth is used, make sure the recipient washes their mouth thoroughly between each test.

Heart witness area.

2. The witness area that we have found to be the most universal and effective is the **Heart Chakra/ Thymus Gland/Sternum (breastbone) point**. This area allows us access in communications with all aspects of the human being: the physical, emotional, mental and spiritual. It is the doorway

to all aspects of the body and can be used to communicate with the body in regards to any substance. This includes medications, vitamins, minerals, herbs, supplements, organic versus inorganic nutrition, water purity, remedies, or objects that you use in daily living (clothes, cosmetics, deodorants, cleaning products, jewelry, crystals, and gemstones etc.). To test these objects, simply have the recipient hold the objects or substance in question over the heart center, palm flat with fingers extended for 10 seconds, hold the question clearly in mind and perform the test. The statement of question to the body and intuition of the recipient would be, "This _____ (sample) is for this person's highest and greatest benefit", or, "At this time or place, this _____ (sample) is for the greatest good of _____ (recipient)."

What can effect your test results?

1. If the arm makes a slight upward jerking movement, instead of weakening or holding the locked-in position, then that means the specific area, substance, or object may have an over-stressing or excessive energy on the individual in question.

2. Take into consideration that the extended arm weakens easily and allow appropriate resting periods.

3. Not all people will have arms that "lock-in" instantly. If the recipient is not weakening with samples of known bad influences you and the individual of the recipient of the test can take a rest by rolling your heads around on your

shoulders in a large circle for 10 clockwise and 10 counterclockwise rotations slowly stretching your neck muscles. The purpose is not only allowing for a rest, but to also assist the muscles and vertebrae in the neck and shoulder region to relax.

4. When the samples are being held during the test at any of the witness areas, make sure their fingers are extended and not pointing towards their body. Always hold the samples with a flat hand because the energy output from the fingertips could disturb the results of the testing.

5. If you are using the abdomen as an witness area, keep in mind that metal buckles or metal zippers can also have an influence on the results of the testing.

Communications in muscle testing involve both the body and the intuition. We have found that the body can be influenced by many different variables in and around the environment in which the testing is being performed. Muscle testing works with the subtle energies and can be easily influenced by some of the following conditions.

Muscle Testing Guidelines: What to do and what to avoid.

1. Test in a room that is light in color.

2. **AVOID ALL FLUORESCENT LIGHTS.**

3. Avoid noises such as music or distracting people.

4. It is best not to have food or gum in your mouth.

5. **Avoid** wearing **synthetic** clothes.

6. **Remove jewelry and metal objects** from both tester and recipient.

7. As a tester, maintain **good emotional and physical health**.

8. The recipient should **always face straight ahead** (both face and eyes).

9. Do not cross feet or hands during a test.

10. **Avoid** standing near or under any **electrical interference** such as T.V. sets.

11. **Always think positive, loving, caring thoughts** towards yourself and the individual being tested. Be neutral as to the objective of the testing.

Your nutritional homeostasis or biochemistry is your own individualized balance that no book, authority or chart can give you. The only way that we have been able to determine the balance for each individual is to test the mind-body for its innate intuitive answers. Different emotions create different energy imbalances within us, and every time we are confronted with a particular emotion, we tend to experience the same pattern. The pain or pattern is a symptom that is the doorway to the subconscious. It is there to remind us that there is a problem. These problems can usually be traced to an emotional experience or trauma, showing us the interrelation of the mind, the muscle, and the organ. Each different illness has a different form of physical patterns. Through muscle testing, you can usually prevent the "disease" by stopping the bodies imbalances before the symptoms manifest into disorder. Muscle testing is a great tool to access the intuitive mind-body knowledge in relationship to the environment and all that is taken in to be for one's highest and greatest benefit.

Part IV
PRACTICE FOR USING YOUR INTUITION

Chapter 11
GET INTUIT

Enjoy learning, practicing and using your intuitive abilities. By using what you have learned in this book, you can achieve an accurate and effective intuition. Enjoy the process of becoming more intuitive as you develop your abilities for creative visualization and knowing. As you grow, you will continue to receive strength and support from this intuitive relationship.

There are three basic ways we can grow:

- We change because we are coerced by society. However, we all agree that is not the best way.

- We change through connections of insight that we make in our minds. Using your intuition to perceive these connections is important. With this awareness you can envision what you truly want, need , or desire.

- We change by understanding the change process itself. Any goals that we wish to achieve are only realized through the change process. **YOU** are the one using the change process during every experience that you have. **YOU** are the one choosing the goal. **YOU** are the one responsible for the results. **YOU** are the one making the decisions. **YOU** are the one acting on those decisions. **YOU** are the one celebrating the results of your success. You will need to decide how you will use your change strategy. You will need to determine your degree of commitment in practicing your intuitive abilities. Your commitment to your process will determine the degree of benefit that you acquire.

Keys to Expanding the Intuition

It is dark before the dawn but the dawn never fails. Trust in the dawn.

There are several elements, or keys, to focus on when you are striving to expand your intuition. Initially, developing these abilities is as simple as paying close *attention* to these subtle feelings that we experience on a regular basis. *Trust* in your expanded abilities, and eliminate the word "coincidence" and the phrase "by accident" from your vocabulary. *Respond* to these intuitive experiences immediately, then learn to *practice* your intuitive abilities as often as possible with *persistence* and *determination*. Finally, *believe* in yourself, and in the source of your information which is the Divine Power, whatever you may perceive that to be. *The degree to which you believe and have confidence in your intuitive mind is the exact degree to which it functions.* If your belief is total, then your intuition functions totally and consciously; If half, then half; If 10%, then only 10% of the time. **What You Believe Will Be.** It is totally controlled by your own mind.

The Eight Elements of the Intuition are:

- **Ask**....the Infinite part of your being to assist you in your Knowingness.

- **Balance**... of the mental and emotional mind.

- **Intention**... of your objective with clarity.

- **Attention**... to recognition of your intuitive experiences.

- **Respond**... to your intuitive experiences immediately. Timing is essential.

- **Trust**... in your intuitive abilities.

- **Persistence**... and Determination with Practice.

- **Believe**... your Knowing Infinite Intelligence.

Creator of Change

Practice using the above keys consciously and deliberately while gaining confidence in your creative ability to change. Applying your intuitive abilities to your daily experiences will assist you in the on-going process of change. As you reflect on your intuitive growth, I suggest that you not always focus on immediate results. Stay in the presence and see how effectively you have been able to practice the eight key elements of the intuition process.

It's normal for us to have some set-backs while developing intuitive abilities, especially during stress or states of imbalance. Don't give up. In your mind go back to times of your intuitive success and acknowledge your knowingness. The goal is to be aware of your knowingness under any circumstance. You will develop and use your intuitive skills at a rate of progress that is just perfect for you. Be patient. As it has been said, "don't push the river".

In using the techniques and the strategies given in this book, remember to decide on a regular daily time to "check in" to see how everything is going or how your developing intuitive abilities are working.

Tune in and ask yourself:

- what new information did I discover?

- did I act on it?

- was I conscious of my breathing?

- what kind of vibrations did I feel?

- what changes do I need to make?

- who would be the best person to assist me?

- have I come closer to fulfilling my goal?

As you develop, quite often you will find yourself relying on your intuition for creative problem solving. This is especially true with our world moving towards an interglobal relationship in which we will be exposed to continual change that will require our intuitions to know what is really going on. We as consumers will also be needing to know how to gauge whether a particular product or service is for our greatest benefit, or if the purchase of a particular product is for the good of our economy or environment.

Two of today's most precious human resources that one can develop are decisive problem solving skills, and time management (how to use your time better). Both can be learned more easily and effectively by using your intuitive consciousness. You will see things as they truly are, not as they seem.

Change is inevitable, but growing and learning from change is optional. Knowing your intuitive mind will assist you in your personal growth and change. As you use your intuitive mind, you will have greater access to your full potential or the level of genius. Celebrate your intuitive journey!

Genius Capacity

The Genius Within Me Is Now Released... I Now fulfill My Destiny.

Creativity cannot be forced, but each one of us is a genius, and has the capability to function at genius level, regardless of past education, IQ, or past experiences. The most important thing is to believe that you have this capability and plug into your intuitive mind. This intuitive capacity is stimulated by a completely *calm, confident, expectant faith* in your own ability to solve your problems and achieve your goals. The more clearly and precisely your goals are presented, and the more committed you are to accomplishing them, the more rapidly the intuitive capacity will work to impel or project those goals into your life.

What are the abilities that geniuses have that create this level of consciousness?

1. The ability to *concentrate single mindedly* on one problem at a time, without diversion or distraction. This is one of the outstanding characteristics among all geniuses.

2. Geniuses have open minds that are *flexible and adaptable* to all the possible ways of approaching a problem, situation, or question. They have *fluidity* in their thinking, and refrain from jumping to conclusions or being dogmatic about any point. They are capable of letting go of one solution for another. Think of a child walking in a garden, and, with a sense of wonder, picking up one flower and then putting it down for another. Such a flexible, adaptable mind is a commonality among geniuses.

3. Geniuses have a *systematic* method for solving every problem with a step-by-step approach. They are able to *isolate* each part of the problem or situation and work progressively in each area. *All problems have a workable solution* so look for it. Change the language from *negative to positive.* For example, rather than calling it a problem with a negative connotation, call it a situation, or a challenge, or an opportunity. When we call something a problem, it causes us to tense up, and this impairs our ability to use all of the parts of our brain to effectively approach and ultimately solve the situation.

When the subconscious mind is stimulated by positive emotions, the effect is of lifting the individual above the horizon of ordinary thought. This permits a distance, scope, and quality of thought not available on the lower plane. This state can sometimes be observed when one is completely absorbed in the solution of a personal or business problem or routine. When lifted to this higher level of thought through mind enhancement of one form or another, an individual occupies relatively the same state of mind as one who has ascended in a jet plane. This vantage point allows one to see over and beyond the horizon line of limits in vision while wrestling with the normal problems of gaining the three basic necessities of food, clothing, and shelter.

> *While on this exalted plane of thought, the creative faculty of the mind gives you freedom for action. Your conscious mind becomes more receptive to ideas which would not normally be heard. You have the ability to develop your intuition. How well you use your intuitive mind is the difference between functioning at your greatest potential, that of genius capacity, or that of an ordinary person using a trial-and-error approach to life.*

Conclusion

In working with the intuition there is usually the feeling of having seen the bigger picture, and how it all fits perfectly together for that person or situation, regardless of how it may appear at the moment. The choices that you, or the individual being tested, have made about certain life experiences become apparent. It is a matter of seeing all of the options clearly, and choosing accurately the one option that will be for your highest and greatest benefit, and will bring you on course with your life's purpose, desires or goals.

You have been provided with many tools of the intuition. It is a good idea to keep a logbook to record the results of your exercises, tests and experiments. In this way progress can be noted and the areas that need work will be revealed. The record can also help you to discover the area in which you are the most accurate or proficient. On a personal note, a record book will also reveal a great deal about your own personal growth through your expanded abilities and beliefs.

Along with these abilities comes the responsibility of knowing what to do with the information or answers you receive. Having access to this infinite knowing and what is or is not appropriate to pass on to others is of utmost importance. Look to your intuition to determine what information is appropriate to share. Do not let your ego interfere. If the information comes from the ego, for example, "look at me, everyone, I have psychic abilities to know everything", then this great skill will be reduced to the level of a parlor game in which the accuracy of the skill will be reduced drastically, possibly bringing about alienation from others, with unhappiness and disappointment being the end result.

Utilizing the Intuition with the intention of helping another person is much easier than you would think. With their permission, you can tune into another person anywhere in the world. The main ingredient is your intention. If you are operating from the proper perspective, with an open heart and a loving, caring intention, you will help yourself and others, to determine what it is that needs to be known in life's quest. Keeping yourself focused from your heart and brow center, with your intention always for the highest and greatest benefit of others, gives you a protective barrier of love and light that will allow you free access to the Infinite.

The intuition serves as a bridge between your conscious self and the Infinite Intelligence, the life force of all creation. I have attempted to impart some tools and practical wisdom to assist you in every day living. If used properly the tools and the intuition will teach you how to improve your quality of life ten-fold.

By knowing your intuitive mind, you can come to know and understand yourself better in the realms of existence that span your physical, mental, emotional and spiritual realities. By knowing your intuitive mind, you can relate more fully to the source of creation. Practice the techniques in this book and let the tools, and your intuition, teach you what is for your highest and greatest good. In all that you do, let it be of benefit to humanity and life in all of it's forms.

If In Doubt, Check It Out.

Be Free Now to Create a Happy and Healthy Future

If you are in need of assistance from unresolved life experiences, dysfunctions, disorders, addictions or destructive habits, know that help can be a phone call away. TRANSFORMational Therapy is an intuitively guided process that promotes healing from trauma and injury, both emotionally and physically by releasing the cause of the problem from the core level. Dale offers himself as a guide to assist you in finding the original cause behind the presenting problem. His remarkable ability to help individuals rewrite their life scripts at a core level can truly create a profound and positive state of being. If you feel that it is time for you to reconnect with your source of truth, personal empowerment, self-esteem and love, Dale provides a safe, caring and supportive space for your process to unfold. This is a safe and gentle process that works deeply, leaving you feeling centered, calm, relaxed and emotionally clear.

For Intuitive Telephone Consultations and Therapy
Call (503) 683-8418 Visa/MC

To Write to the Author

We cannot guarantee that every letter written to the author can be answered, but all will be forwarded. Both the author and the publisher appreciate hearing from readers, hoping for your enjoyment and personal benefit from this book. The author sometimes participates in seminars and workshops, and dates and places are announced in the Crystalline Seminar quarterly bulletins. To write to the author with your intuitive experiences, to ask a question, or to be put on the bulletin mailing list, write to:

Dale W. Olson
Crystalline Publications
P.O. Box 2088
Eugene, OR 97402
U.S.A.

Bibliography

Archdale, F.A., **Elementary Radiesthesia, and the Use of the Pendulum**. The British Society of Dowsers, 1950.

Beasse, Pierre, **A New and Rational Treatise of Dowsing according to the methods of Physical Radiethesie.** Mokelumne Hill, Ca.:Health Research, 1975.

Bentov, Itzhak, **Stalking The Wild Pendulum**. N.Y.:E.P. Dutton, 1977.

Besant, A., & Leadbeater, C.W., **Thought-Forms.** Il.:Theosophical Publishing House, 1971.

Bhattacharyya, Benoytosh, **Magnet Dowsing**. Calcutta, India:Firma K.L. Mukhopadhyay, 1967.

Bhattacharyya, Benoytosh, **The Science of Cosmic Ray Therapy or Teletherapy.** Calcutta, India:Firma KLM Private LTD, 1976.

Biokinesiology Institute, **Take Care of Yourselves Naturally.** Biokinesiology Institute, 1984.

Bird, C.,& Tompkins, P., **The Secret Life Of Plants.**
N.Y.:Avon Books, 1973.

Bird, Christopher, "Dowsing in the United States of America:
History, Past Achievements and Current Research."
The American Dowser, vol 13, no.3, August, 1973, pp.
105-6.

Bird, Christopher, "Finding It by Dowsing," **Psychic,** Vol.VI,
no.4, September/October, 1975. pp. 8-13.

Blackburn, Gabriele, **The Science and Art of the Pendulum:
A Complete Course in Radiethesia.** Idylwild Books,
1983.

Brennan, Barbara Ann, Hands Of Light: **A Guide to Healing
Through the Human Energy Field.** Bantam Books,
1987.

Cameron, Verne L., **Map Dowsing.** Elsinore, Ca:El Cariso
Publications, 1971.

Chapman, E.C., **The 12 Tissue Salts.** Jove Publications 1979.

Cayce, Edgar, **Auras.** ARE Press, 1945.

Davis Ph.D., Albert Roy, **The Anatomy of Biomagnetism.**
Fl.:Davis Research.

De La Warr, G., **Matter in the Making.** London:Vincent Stuart Ltd., 1966.

Finch, W.J., **The Pendulum & Possession.** AZ.:Esoteric Publications, 1975.

Gardner, Joy, **Color and Crystals: A Journey Through the Chakras.** Ca.:The Crossing Press 1988.

Graves, Tom, **Dowsing and Archaeology.** Turnstone Press, 1980.

Hay, Louise L., **You Can Heal Your Life.** Ca.:Hay House, 1984.

Hay, LouiseL., **Heal Your Body.** Ca.:Hay House, 1982.

Judith, Anodea, **Wheels of Life.** MN:Liewellyn Publications, 1987.

Leadbeater, C.W., **The Chakras.** London: Theosophical Publishing House, 1974.

Lorusso Julia, and Glick Joel, **"Healing Stoned," The Therapeutic Use of Gems and Minerals.** Brotherhood of Life, 1983.

Massy Ph.D., Robert, **You are What You Breathe: The Negative Ion Story.** CO:University of the Trees Press, 1980.

McCamy, Jean, **"Witching for Water"**, Mother Earth News,
No. 6, Nov., 1970, p.76.

Mermet, Abbe', **Principles and Practice of Radiesthesia.**
London:Watkins Publishers, 1935.

Moss, T., Probability of the Impossible: **Scientific Discoveries
and Explorations in the Psychic World.** Ca.:J.P.
Tarcher, 1974.

Nielsen, Greg & Polansky, Joseph, **Pendulum Power.**
Excalibur Books, 1982.

Ostrander, Sheila & Schroeder, Lynn, **Psychic Discoveries
Behind the Iron Curtain.** Bantam Books, 1971.

Ramacharaka, Yogi, **Science of Breath.** Yogi Publication
Society, 1904.

Raphaell, Katrina, **Crystal Enlightenment.** Aurora Press,
1986.

Raphaell, Katrina, **Crystal Healing.** Aurora Press, 1987.

Roberts, Kenneth. **Henry Gross and His Dowsing Rod.**
N.Y.:Doubleday, 1951.

Shinn, Florence, **The Power of the Spoken Word.** DeVorss & Co., 1945.

Shinn, Florence, **The Game of Life and How to Play it.** Devorss & Co., 1925.

Shinn, Florence, **Your Word is Your Wand.** DeVorss & Co., 1928.

The American Dowser, Vermont: American Society of Dowsers, 1960-1975

Vogel, Marcel, *Psychic Research Newsletter.* Ca.:Psychic Research, 1974-1990.

Wayland, Bruce & Shirley, **Steps to Dowsing Power.** Life Force Press, Inc., 1976.

KNOWING YOUR INTUITIVE MIND
BOOKS AND TOOLS

Additional material available through Crystalline Publications: Knowing Your Intuitive Mind, Advanced Pendulum Instruction & Applications, and Pendulum Charts. Also available, crystal pendulums and brass dowsing rods.

QUANTITY		UNIT PRICE	TOTAL PRICE
_____	**Knowing Your Intuitive Mind** by Dale W. Olson	$14.95	_____
_____	Knowing Your Intuitive Mind: **Advanced Pendulum Instruction & Applications** by Dale W. Olson	$11.95	_____
_____	Knowing Your Intuitive Mind: **Pendulum Charts** by Dale W. Olson	$9.95	_____

PENDULUMS (natural quartz crystals with copper setting)

_____	Large Pendulum (1¼"+)	$12.95	_____
_____	Small Pendulums (1" -)	$9.95	_____

DOWSING RODS (brass with clear handles)

_____	Large 16" set dowsing rods	$12.95	_____
_____	Small 12" set dowsing rods	$9.95	_____

BOOK/PENDULUM CHART SETS
with Pendulum & Dowsing Rods

_____ Advanced Pendulum Instruction &
Applications, Pendulum Charts,
Small Pendulum, Small Rods $35.95   _____

_____ Advanced Pendulum Instruction &
Applications, Pendulum Charts,
Large Pendulum, Large Rods $40.95   _____

_____ Knowing Your Intuitive Mind Book,
Advanced Pendulum Instruction &
Applications, Pendulum Charts,
Small Pendulum, Small Rods $50.95   _____

_____ Knowing Your Intuitive Mind Book,
Advanced Pendulum Instruction &
Applications, Pendulum Charts,
Large Pendulum, Large Rods $55.95   _____

(40% discount for stores)   **Subtotal**   _____

              Shipping + 12% ($2.75 minimum)   _____

                                        Total   _____

Name_____

Address _____

City _____ State _____ Zip _____

Telephone (   )_____

✔ check on   ☐ Check   ☐ Money Order   ☐ Visa™   ☐ MasterCard™

Charge Card # _____ Exp. Date _____

☐ I would like to know about future seminars.
☐ I would like information about sponsoring an intuition seminar.

Send to: Crystalline Publications
P.O. Box 2088 • Eugene, OR 97402

Telephone Orders: Visa™ and MasterCard™ only
Call (503) 683-8418
1-800-688-8418